INSURANCE BAD FAITH:

The Law in Georgia
Second Edition

By

James (Jay) Sadd
Richard E. Dolder
Samantha Johnson

SLAPPEY & SADD, LLC

352 Sandy Springs Circle
Atlanta, GA 30328
(404) 255-6677
(888) 474-9616

www.lawyersatlanta.com

16 15 14 13   1 2 3 4 5

Printed in the United States of America

ISBN 978-0-615-41297-9

PREFACE TO THE SECOND EDITION

We have been flattered to receive many inquiries from both the defense and plaintiffs' bar concerning the definition of "bad faith", what to do if an insurance company has acted in bad faith, and the practical implications of handling bad-faith cases at various stages of both the underlying case and the following bad-faith case against the insurance company. Following publication of the first edition, the inquiries increased. As we wrote in the preface to that first edition, the questions and concerns raised continue to be interesting, educational and sometimes downright confounding.

As our insurance-coverage and bad-faith practices have grown, we achieve immense satisfaction from helping our clients, be it the physician whose insurer refuses to settle a potentially explosive malpractice case, a small business denied coverage following a fire, or just about any business or individual who, at the end of a lawsuit, contemplates the financial and emotional devastation caused by an excess judgment as their insurer walks away. In the context of a bad-faith case under the common law, our satisfaction is made all the more complete when by way of making our client, the insured, whole, the judgment against the insured is satisfied in full.

We hope that you will continue to feel free to give us a call any time you have questions or ideas to discuss regarding insurance coverage or possible insurer bad faith. We enjoy the discussions and continue to consider it a privilege to represent policyholders in cases involving insurer bad faith and other insurance-related disputes. Our experience in formerly representing insurance companies has given us a perspective that allows us to help attorneys who infrequently deal with insurance law. Our philosophy has always been to share, as others sharing with us has certainly contributed to where we are today. To which we again say – thank you.

Jay Sadd
Rich Dolder

ABOUT THE AUTHORS

James (Jay) Sadd is a founding member of Slappey & Sadd, LLC, Atlanta, Georgia. Jay formed Slappey & Sadd in 1992 with Scott Slappey to represent families, workers and consumers who have been critically injured or lost a loved one because of the negligence or willful conduct of others. Jay was lead counsel for 37 victims of the 1996 Centennial Olympic Park bombing, and he has successfully represented many other victims and families who have been mistreated by insurance companies or suffered catastrophic injuries or wrongful death. He was lead counsel on the case of *Thomas v. Atlanta Cas. Co.*, 253 Ga. App. 199, 558 S.E. 2d 432 (2001), an insurance bad-faith case that resulted in a $5.6 million verdict in 2006.

Jay began his legal career in insurance and product-liability defense with Freeman & Hawkins in Atlanta. For the last 21 years, his practice has been devoted to representing plaintiffs, while often taking cases against various insurance companies.

Jay practices in every court of Georgia, the United States District Courts of Georgia and the United States Court of Appeals for the 11th Circuit. He is licensed to practice in West Virginia, where he was born and reared.

Jay holds a Juris Doctorate from the Walter F. George School of Law, Mercer University, 1987. He is a member of the State Bar of Georgia, Atlanta Bar Association, Atlanta Lawyers Club, Georgia Trial Lawyers Association, American Association for Justice, West Virginia Bar Association, Sandy Springs Bar Association, and the DeKalb Bar Association.

Jay has been named a Top 100 Georgia Super Lawyer in *Atlanta* magazine and *Georgia Super Lawyers Magazine*® as well as being named by *Georgia Trend* Magazine as among Georgia's "Legal Elite" many times. His law firm has been recognized as "Best Lawyers" by US News and World Report. Jay is a Fellow of the Lawyers Foundation of Georgia, an honor that recognizes those lawyers whose public and private careers demonstrate outstanding legal abilities and a devotion to their communities.

He holds the highest rating possible (AV Preeminent) by Martindale-Hubble/LexisNexis. Jay lives in Atlanta, with his wife, Laura, and two children.

ABOUT THE AUTHORS

Richard E. Dolder is a partner at the law firm of Slappey & Sadd. LLC, where he represents individuals and businesses who are denied coverage improperly or have been treated unfairly by their insurance companies. Early in his career, Rich worked for a national law firm that specialized in representing certain underwriters in the insurance market at Lloyds of London. Previous to joining Slappey & Sadd, he practiced with an international law firm that represented Fortune 500 companies in coverage disputes with their insurance companies.

Rich has provided legal advice on the issue of insurance coverage in varied situations, including a liability insurer's duty to defend, a property insurer alleging arson, a railroad's liability for polluted land, mold damage to a hotel, liability coverage for allegations of slander and defamation, life insurance benefits, disability benefits, liability coverage for contractors accused of improper workmanship, an excess carrier's duty to the primary insurer, and trucking and auto coverage.

He has defended and prosecuted numerous lawsuits involving allegations of insurance bad faith, both under the common law and under OCGA § 33-4-6. He has been designated as an expert witness with regard to awards of attorneys' fees under that statute.

Rich also counsels individuals, businesses and other attorneys in insurance issues not requiring litigation, including what to do when insurance companies delay payment on valid claims, standing by insureds subjected to Examinations Under Oath and providing honest and thoughtful evaluations of various insurance issues.

Rich graduated from the University of Florida College of Law in 1998. He has been designated a Super Lawyer by *Georgia Super Lawyers Magazine*®.

ABOUT THE AUTHORS

Samantha Johnson is an Associate General Counsel for Grady Health System, one of the largest public academic healthcare systems in the United States. She advises, counsels, and educates hospital employees and medical staff regarding patient care, ethics, human resources, compliance, and regulatory matters; drafts and reviews contracts, agreements, and policies; represents Grady in litigation in the state and federal courts of Georgia and in administrative matters before Georgia Department of Labor and U.S. Equal Employment Opportunity Commission; and manages outside attorneys in the handling of litigation files.

After a two and a half year internship in Grady's legal department while a student at the Georgia State University College of Law, Samantha practiced for six years as an insurance coverage and litigation attorney with the Atlanta firms of Mabry & McClelland, LLP and Goodman, McGuffey, Lindsey & Johnson, LLP. She was twice named a Georgia Super Lawyers Rising Star. She counseled and represented insurance companies, policyholders, and additional insureds in matters concerning coverage under commercial general liability, automobile, homeowners', umbrella/excess, and workers' compensation insurance policies and litigated numerous bad faith actions on behalf of both policyholders and insurers. She also practiced as a contract attorney with Slappey & Sadd, LLC, where she assisted the attorneys on complex insurance bad faith matters.

Samantha is a contributing author of two chapters ("Ethical Issues for Insurance Defense Counsel" and "Vendors/Vendees") for the American Bar Association's *Handbook on Additional Insureds* (Michael Menapace, et al., ed., 2012).

Samantha is an active member of both the State Bar of Georgia and the State Bar of South Carolina. A native of Atlanta, Georgia, she is a graduate of The Westminster Schools (1996), Vanderbilt University (B.A. with honors in English; B.A. psychology, 2000) and the Georgia State University College of Law (J.D., 2003). She is currently pursuing her professional Masters of Business Administration and Masters of Health Administration at the J. Mack Robinson College of Business at Georgia State University and will graduate in 2014.

INTRODUCTION

The Promise of Peace of Mind

To an economist, insurance is a financial mechanism that has historically benefited society by fueling economic growth. Thus, in the 17th century, insurance agreements underwritten in Edward Lloyd's Coffee House in London allowed investors to spread the risk of sending ships across dangerous seas, sparking a wave of exploration and world trade. Today, property policies expand the availability of home mortgages, because an insured home reduces a lender's risk of a total loss by fire or other casualty.

To a businessperson, insurance is commerce. Like any commercial enterprise, its goal is to make money. To do so, insurance companies collect premiums from many insureds in a greater amount than they will pay out in claims. Under a more modern model, the business of insurance is designed to hold onto the premium long enough so that the income earned by invested premiums exceeds amounts paid out in claims over time.

Of course, insurance is something more than a historical phenomenon, financial mechanism or method of commerce. *Insurance is a promise.* A promise to rebuild a house that burns. A promise to pay benefits to a disabled worker. A promise to protect an insured who accidentally causes injury to others in an automobile accident. In short, insurance is the promise of peace of mind. As insurers tell us in their advertising, insurance cannot stop bad things from happening, but it can reduce the negative impact and turn a potentially ruinous situation into a manageable risk.

Like all promises, the promise of peace of mind is sometimes broken. This book addresses the law applicable to those situations where the insurer not only breaks the promise, but does so negligently or in "bad faith."

Georgia recognizes two species of bad faith specific to insurance companies. The first is sometimes referred to as statutory bad faith and addresses an insurance company's failure to pay money due on a valid claim. Statutory bad faith deals primarily with the promise of the insurer to indemnify. The second is referred to as common-law bad faith and deals with the promise of an insurer to protect its insured from the threat of legal liability and the hazards of litigation. An insurer fulfills that promise by using its litigation expertise, investigative resources and prudent discretion in the claims-handling process and during the course of litigation to guard the insured against any liability, and particularly liability in excess of policy limits.

Although distinctly different, both species of bad faith involve interpretation of insurance policies. Accordingly, Chapter 1 serves as an introduction to the rules of contract interpretation as applied to insurance contracts. Chapters 2 and 3 explain the specific elements and application of statutory and common-law bad faith, respectively. Because this book is intended to aid the legal practitioner, Chapter 4 summarizes the procedure applicable to bad-faith lawsuits, and Chapter 5 addresses several of the recurring issues common to bad-faith lawsuits. Chapter 6 focuses on ethical issues that arise among lawyers representing insurers, insureds and claimants. Chapter 7, new to this edition, addresses liability by insurance agents and brokers for "negligent procurement," a claim often ancillary to allegations of insurer bad faith.

CHAPTER 1

CONSTRUCTION AND INTERPRETATION OF INSURANCE CONTRACTS

CHAPTER 2

STATUTORY BAD FAITH

CHAPTER 3

COMMON-LAW BAD FAITH

CHAPTER 4

PROCEDURAL ASPECTS OF BAD-FAITH CASES

CHAPTER 5

SPECIAL ISSUES IN INSURANCE LITIGATION

CHAPTER 6

ETHICAL ISSUES IN INSURANCE PRACTICE

CHAPTER 7

NEGLIGENT PROCUREMENT

CHAPTER 1

CONSTRUCTION AND INTERPRETATION
OF INSURANCE CONTRACTS

§ 1.1 INTRODUCTION

Because an insurance policy is a contract, any dispute implicating an insurer's bad faith will involve the meaning of the words in the insurance policy. This is true no matter the type of bad faith at issue. Construction and interpretation of an insurance policy come into play in statutory bad-faith cases brought under O.C.G.A. § 33-4-6 (which are addressed in detail in Chapter 2) as well as in bad-faith cases under the common law (which are addressed in detail in Chapter 3). With respect to statutory bad faith, for example, an insurer may eventually be deemed to have withheld payment of policy proceeds in bad faith because the claim was clearly covered under the plain terms of the insurance policy.[1] On the other hand, an insurer may be deemed to have not acted in bad faith under the statute even though its interpretation of the policy was later determined to be incorrect, but only if the question of interpretation is objectively a "close question."[2] With respect to the common law, a bad-faith claim may have its genesis in the insurer's refusal to settle a claim or defend a lawsuit it believes not to be covered, leading to a default judgment in excess of policy limits. Thus, an insured who brings a bad-faith, failure-to-settle claim may, in some

---

[1] *See, e.g., Rentrite, Inc. v. Sentry Select Ins. Co.*, 293 Ga. App. 643, 648, 667 S.E.2d 888, 892 (2008) (finding that insured may sustain bad-faith cause of action based, in part, on the insurer's representation to its insured and to the court that coverage was voided for the insured's failure to fulfill certain requirements even though the plain language of the policy demonstrated that it contained no such requirements).

[2] *Schoen v. Atlanta Cas. Co.*, 200 Ga. App. 109, 110, 407 S.E.2d 91, 92 (1991) (interpreting policy in favor of coverage but finding no bad faith because issue of interpretation was a "close question").

instances, be required to show that there is coverage under the insurance contract. Knowledge of the rules of contract construction as applied to insurance policies is obviously necessary, therefore, to correctly analyze and effectively litigate situations involving the potential bad faith of an insurer under O.C.G.A. § 33-4-6 as well as under the common law.

§ 1.2   THE RULE OF PLAIN MEANING

The insurer and the insured are bound by the plain and unambiguous terms of the insurance contract.[3] In construing a contract, a court first "determine[s] if the instrument's language is clear and unambiguous."[4] "If the language is unambiguous, the court simply enforces the contract according to the terms, and looks to the contract alone for the meaning."[5]

The plain terms of an unambiguous policy are given full effect even though they are beneficial to the insurer and detrimental to the insured.[6] The cardinal rule of contract construction is to ascertain the parties' intent, so that when the terms of the contract are clear and unambiguous, the court

---

[3]   *Hurst v. Grange Mut. Cas. Co.*, 266 Ga. 716, 470 S.E.2d 659 (1996), citing *Richards v. Hanover Ins. Co.*, 250 Ga. 613, 299 S.E.2d 561 (1983).

[4]   *Am. Empire Surplus Lines Ins. Co. v. Hathaway Dev. Co., Inc.*, 288 Ga. 749, 750, 707 S.E.2d 369, 371 (2011).

[5]   *Am. Empire Surplus Lines Ins. Co. v. Hathaway Dev. Co., Inc.*, 288 Ga. 749, 750, 707 S.E.2d 369, 371 (2011).

[6]   "As is true with all contracts, unambiguous terms in an insurance policy require no construction, and their plain meaning will be given full effect, regardless of whether they might be of benefit to the insurer, or be of detriment to an insured." *Payne v. Twiggs County School Dist.*, 269 Ga. 361, 363, 496 S.E.2d 690 (1998). *See also Continental Cas. Co. v. H.S.I. Financial Services, Inc.*, 266 Ga. 260, 262, 466 S.E.2d 4 (1996); *Truitt Oil & Gas Co. v. Ranger Ins. Co.*, 231 Ga. App. 89, 90, 498 S.E.2d 572 (1998); *Littrell v. Colony Ins. Co.*, 228 Ga. App. 552, 553, 492 S.E.2d 299 (1997); *Cotton States Mut. Ins. Co. v. Hipps*, 224 Ga. App. 756, 757, 481 S.E.2d 876 (1997); *Al Who Enterprises, Inc. v. Capitol Indem. Corp.*, 217 Ga. App. 423, 426, 457 S.E.2d 696 (1995); *St. Paul Fire & Marine Ins. Co. v. Mose Gordon Const. Co.*, 121 Ga. App. 33, 34-35, 172 S.E.2d 459 (1970).

looks to the contract alone to determine that intent.[7] Construction and interpretation of contracts are generally matters of law for the court.[8]

Unless otherwise defined in the contract, terms in an insurance policy are given their ordinary and customary meaning.[9] Courts sometimes use dictionaries to determine the "ordinary and customary meaning" of words. For example, in *Western Pacific Mut. Ins. Co. v. Davies*, the Court of Appeals looked to a dictionary to determine the definition of "failure."[10] The Court of Appeals stated that "[i]n construing a contract of insurance to ascertain the intent of the parties, the court should give a term or phrase in the contract its ordinary meaning or common signification as defined by dictionaries, because they supply the plain, ordinary, and popular sense unless the words are terms of art."[11]

---

[7] *ALEA London Ltd. v. Woodcock*, 286 Ga. App. 572, 576, 649 S.E.2d 740 (2007), citing *North Metro Directories Publishing v. Cotton States Mut. Ins. Co.*, 279 Ga. App. 492, 494(1), 631 S.E.2d 726 (2006); O.C.G.A. § 13-2-3.

[8] O.C.G.A. § 13-2-1; *ALEA London Ltd. v. Woodcock*, 286 Ga. App. 572, 576, 649 S.E.2d 740, 744-45 (2007) (finding that ambiguity exists but disagreeing with trial court's decision to send issue to the jury because "[i]f the court finds that an ambiguity exists, it is the court's duty to resolve that ambiguity by applying the pertinent rules of contract construction"). *Old Republic Union Ins. Co. v. Floyd Beasley & Sons, Inc.*, 250 Ga. App. 673, 675, 551 S.E.2d 388 (2001). *See also Guest v. Horace Mann Ins. Co.*, 168 Ga. App. 714, 715, 310 S.E.2d 241 (1983) ("interpretation of the provisions of a plain and definite policy of insurance is a matter of law for the courts"); *Georgia Farm Bureau Mut. Ins. Co. v. Jackson*, 240 Ga. App. 127, 522 S.E.2d 716 (1999); *Southern General Ins. Co. v. Alford*, 234 Ga. App. 615, 616, 507 S.E.2d 179 (1998).

[9] *Western Pacific Mut. Ins. Co. v. Davies*, 267 Ga. App. 675, 678, 601 S.E.2d 363 (2004), citing *Stagl v. Assurance Co. of America*, 245 Ga. App. 8, 10, 539 S.E.2d 173 (2000). See also *Canal Ins. Co. v. Wilkes Supply Co., Inc.*, 203 Ga. App. 35, 36-37, 416 S.E.2d 105 (1992), citing *United States Fire Ins. Co. v. Capitol Ford Truck Sales, Inc.*, 257 Ga. 77, 78-79, 355 S.E.2d 428 (1987), O.C.G.A. § 13-2-2(2), and *Griffin v. Adams*, 175 Ga. App. 715, 716, 334 S.E.2d 42 (1985) ("Insurance contracts are governed by the rules of construction applicable to other contracts and words in the policy must be given their usual and common signification and customary meaning.").

[10] *Western Pacific Mut. Ins. Co. v. Davies*, 267 Ga. App. 675, 678, 601 S.E.2d 363 (2004).

[11] *Id.*, citing O.C.G.A. § 13-2-2(2), *State Farm Fire & Cas. Co. v. American Hardware Mut. Ins. Co.*, 224 Ga. App. 789, 792, 482 S.E.2d 714 (1997) and *Henderson v. Henderson*, 152 Ga. App. 846, 847, 264 S.E.2d 299 (1979).

Courts also look to statutory definitions for an understanding of words not defined in an insurance policy.[12] The practice has its limits, however, and sometimes "[s]uch interweaving of inconsistent definitions of words defined in dictionaries with words defined in statutes is a slender reed upon which to base a clear meaning of a contractual term."[13]

§ 1.3   RULE OF BROAD CONSTRUCTION

"It is a cardinal principle of insurance law that a policy or contract of insurance is to be construed liberally in favor of the insured and strictly as against the insurer."[14] "Under Georgia law, insurance policies are liberally construed in favor of coverage."[15] "When a dispute arises between the insurer and the insured, the policy should be construed liberally in favor of the insured."[16] The policy must be construed as to provide for coverage unless the lack of coverage clearly appears.[17] An insurance policy is construed liberally to provide coverage.[18] Applying Georgia law, the Eleventh Circuit has recognized the same principle, writing that "Georgia courts liberally construe disability policies in favor of insureds and strictly against insurers."[19]

---

[12] *See, Am. Empire Surplus Lines Ins. Co. v. Hathaway Dev. Co., Inc.,* 288 Ga. 749, 753, 707 S.E.2d 369, 372 (2011), Melton, J., dissenting (referring to definition of "accident" contained in OCGA § 1–3–3(2)).

[13] *State Auto Prop. & Cas. Co. v. Matty,* 286 Ga. 611, 612, 690 S.E.2d 614, 616 (2010).

[14] *Clark v. United Ins. Co. of Am.,* 199 Ga. App. 1, 5, 404 S.E.2d 149, 153 (1991).

[15] *Barrett v. Nat'l Union Fire Ins. Co. of Pitt.,* 304 Ga. App. 314, 320-21, 696 S.E.2d 326, 331 (2010).

[16] *Clarke v. UNUM Life Ins. Co. of Am.,* 14 F. Supp. 2d 1351, 1354 (S.D. Ga. 1998), citing *North Am. Ins. Co. v. Watson,* 6 Ga. App. 193, 195, 64 S.E. 693 (1909).

[17] *Comes v. United States,* 918 F. Supp. 382, 384 (M.D. Ga. 1996).

[18] *Auto-Owners Ins. Co. v. Parks,* 278 Ga. App. 444, 447, 629 S.E.2d 118 (2006), citing *Lemieux v. Blue Cross & Blue Shield of Ga. Inc.,* 216 Ga. App. 230, 231, 453 S.E.2d 749 (1994).

[19] *Giddens v. Equitable Life Assur. Soc. of U.S.,* 445 F.3d 1286, 1299-300 (11th Cir. 2006).

The rule of broad construction applies even if there is no ambiguity in the policy. For example, in *Roland v. Georgia Farm Bureau Mut. Ins. Co.*, the Supreme Court of Georgia construed an insurance policy broadly to find coverage without finding any ambiguity.[20] Likewise, the court in *Hartford Cas. Ins. Co. v. Smith* "liberally construed" the grant of coverage and "strictly construed" conditions against the insurer – the drafter – without holding that there was an ambiguity.[21] More recently, the Georgia Court of Appeals in *Barrett v. Nat'l Union Fire Ins. Co. of Pitt.*, noted that the phrase "but for" is interpreted broadly in a coverage provision but narrowly in a provision limiting coverage, even though there was no ambiguity.[22] Federal district courts applying Georgia law have applied the same rule.[23]

§ 1.4   THE REASONABLE EXPECTATIONS DOCTRINE

The plain meaning of an insurance policy is informed by the reasonable expectations of the insured. "A contract of insurance should be strictly construed against the insurer and read in favor of coverage in accordance with the reasonable expectations of the insured."[24] Insurance policies are contracts of adhesion, drawn by insurers, and should be construed as reasonably understood by an insured. The test is not what the insurer intended its words to mean, but rather what a reasonable person in the insured's position would understand them to mean.[25] "The policy should be read as a

---

[20] *Roland v. Georgia Farm Bureau Mut. Ins. Co.*, 265 Ga. 776, 462 S.E.2d 623 (1995).
[21] *Hartford Cas. Ins. Co. v. Smith*, 268 Ga. App. 224, 603 S.E.2d 298 (2004), *cert. denied*, Sept. 27, 2004.
[22] *Barrett v. Nat'l Union Fire Ins. Co. of Pitt.*, 304 Ga. App. 314, 320-21, 696 S.E.2d 326, 331 (2010).
[23] *Clarke v. UNUM Life Ins. Co. of Am.*, 14 F. Supp. 2d 1351, 1354 (S.D. Ga. 1998).
[24] *Roland v. Georgia Farm Bureau Mut. Ins. Co.*, 265 Ga. 776, 777, 462 S.E.2d 623 (1995).
[25] *Rentrite, Inc. v. Sentry Select Ins. Co.*, 293 Ga. App. 643, 647, 667 S.E.2d 888 (2008), citing *First Financial Ins. Co. v. American Sandblasting Co.*,

layman would read it and not as it might be analyzed by an insurance expert or an attorney."[26]

The Supreme Court of Georgia, in *Richards v. Hanover Ins. Co.*, expressly approved application of the reasonable expectations rule and explained its function in conjunction with other rules of policy construction.[27] In *Richards*, a couple's insured home was destroyed by fire. The husband was arrested for arson. The insurance company denied coverage to the wife, relying on an exclusion barring coverage in the event of "neglect of the insured to use all reasonable means to save and preserve property." In essence, the insurer argued that the "neglect provision" created a joint obligation by both insureds to preserve the property, and that if one insured breached the obligation the exclusion was triggered for both. The wife argued that her duty under the "neglect provision" was several from that of her husband's. The Georgia Supreme Court agreed, not by relying on public policy or concepts of fairness, but by reference to the plain terms of the policy construed in light of the insured's reasonable expectations. The court looked to the definition of "insured," and found that the term referred to an individual. Furthermore, reading the definition in light of the reasonable expectations of the insured, nothing in the language of the policy would indicate to a reasonable insured that the "neglect provision" created a joint – as opposed to several – obligation.

§ 1.5   Exclusions, Exceptions and Limitations Narrowly Construed

In contrast to the grant of coverage in an insurance policy, exceptions and exclusions to coverage must be narrowly and

---

223 Ga. App. 232, 477 S.E.2d 390 (1996) and *Western Pacific Mut. Ins. Co. v. Davies*, 267 Ga. App. 675, 680, 601 S.E.2d 363 (2004).

[26] *Continental Ins. Co. v. American Motorist Ins. Co.*, 247 Ga. App. 331, 334-335, 542 S.E.2d 607, 610 (1990).

[27] *Richards v. Hanover Ins. Co.*, 250 Ga. 613, 299 S.E.2d 561 (1983).

strictly construed against the insurer and liberally construed in favor of the insured to afford coverage.[28] A contract of insurance is construed most strongly against the insurer and liberally in favor of the insured, particularly where the insurer seeks to deny coverage based upon a policy exclusion.[29] Exceptions, limitations and exclusions to insuring agreements require a narrow construction on the theory that the insurer, having affirmatively expressed coverage through broad promises, assumes a duty to define any limitations on that coverage in clear and explicit terms.[30] Where an insurer grants coverage to an insured, any exclusions from coverage must be defined clearly and distinctly.[31] Exclusions are strictly construed.[32]

§ 1.6   AMBIGUITIES

Under the rule of *contra proferentem*, ambiguities in an insurance policy are strictly construed against the insurer and in favor of coverage, under the theory that the insurer drafted the contract.[33] Ambiguity exists when a term,

---

[28] *Hartford Cas. Ins. Co. v. Smith*, 268 Ga. App. 224, 227, 603 S.E.2d 298 (2004) ("Policies of insurance will be liberally construed in favor of the object to be accomplished, and the conditions and provisions of contracts of insurance will be strictly construed against the insurer who prepares such contracts."), *cert. denied*, Sept. 27, 2004.

[29] *Georgia Farm Bureau Mut. Ins. Co. v. Meyers*, 249 Ga. App. 322, 324, 548 S.E.2d 67 (2001).

[30] *Alley v. Great American Ins. Co.*, 160 Ga. App. 597, 600, 287 S.E.2d 613 (1981). *See also Rentrite, Inc. v. Sentry Select Ins. Co.*, 294 Ga. App. 643, 647, 667 S.E.2d 888, 892 (2008) ("exclusions in an insurance policy are to be interpreted narrowly, in favor of the insured, on the theory that the insurer, having affirmatively expressed coverage through broad promises, assumes a duty to define any limitations on that coverage in clear and explicit terms"); *Fidelity Nat'l Title Ins. Co. v. Matrix Financial Services Co.*, 255 Ga. App. 874, 878, 567 S.E.2d 96, 100 (2002) (exclusions are construed strongly against the insurer and in favor of coverage).

[31] *Hurst v. Grange Mut. Cas. Co.*, 266 Ga. 712, 716, 470 S.E.2d 659 (1996).

[32] *Travelers Indem. Co. v. Whalley Const. Co.*, 160 Ga. App. 438, 440, 287 S.E.2d 226 (1981).

[33] *Richards v. Hanover Ins. Co.*, 250 Ga. 613, 615, 299 S.E.2d 561, 564 (1983), citing *Hulsey v. Interstate Life & Accident Ins. Co.*, 207 Ga. 167, 169, 60 S.E.2d 353 (1950). *See also Anderson v. Southeastern Fidelity Ins. Co.*, 251 Ga.

phrase, or section "may be fairly construed in more than one way."[34] An ambiguity involves a choice between two or more constructions of the contract.[35] In *Georgia Farm Bureau Mut. Ins. Co. v. Meyers,*[36] the Court of Appeals explained:

> Ambiguity in an insurance contract is duplicity, indistinctiveness, uncertainty of meaning of expression, and words or phrases which cause uncertainty of meaning and may be fairly construed in more than one way. Where a term of a policy of insurance is susceptible to two or more constructions, even when such multiple constructions are all logical and reasonable, such term is ambiguous and will be strictly construed against the insurer as the drafter and in favor of the insured. Where the phrasing of the policy is so confusing that an average policyholder cannot make out the boundaries of coverage, the policy is genuinely ambiguous.

Whether or not an ambiguity exists in an insurance policy is a matter of law for the court to decide.[37] In determining whether the terms of the policy are subject to more than one reasonable interpretation, the policy should be read as a layman would read it and not as an insurance expert or an attorney might analyze it.[38] A clause in an insurance policy

556, 557, 307 S.E.2d 499 (1983) ("[a]n ambiguity in a document should be construed against its draftsman") *and* O.C.G.A. § 13-2-2(5).

[34] *Georgia Farm Bureau Mut. Ins. Co. v. Meyers,* 249 Ga. App. 322, 324, 548 S.E.2d 67 (2001).

[35] *Western Pacific Mut. Ins. Co. v. Davies,* 267 Ga. App. 675, 680, 601 S.E.2d 363 (2004), citing *Burden v. Thomas,* 104 Ga. App. 300, 302, 121 S.E.2d 684 (1961).

[36] *Georgia Farm Bureau Mut. Ins. Co. v. Meyers,* 249 Ga. App. 322, 324, 548 S.E.2d 67 (2001).

[37] *Banks v. Brotherhood Mut. Ins. Co.,* 301 Ga. App. 101, 102, 686 S.E.2d 872 (2009).

[38] *Id.* at 103, 686 S.E.2d 872 citing *State Farm Mut. Auto. Ins. Co. v. Staton,* 286 Ga. 23, 25, 685 S.E.2d 263 (2009).

deemed unambiguous in one situation may be deemed ambiguous when applied to a different situation.[39]

"Multiple logical interpretations make a clause ambiguous as a matter of law."[40] "[I]f a provision of an insurance contract is susceptible of two or more constructions, even when the multiple constructions are all logical and reasonable, it is ambiguous."[41] "Pursuant to the rule of construction set forth at O.C.G.A. § 13-2-2(5), the contract will be construed strictly against the insurer/drafter and in favor of the insured."[42] If two clauses in an insurance contract are contradictory, an ambiguity is created, and the clause more favorable to the insured will be enforced.[43]

§ 1.7   CONSTRUCTION UPHOLDING WHOLE CONTRACT

The rules of construction require the court to consider the policy as a whole, to give effect to each provision, and to interpret each provision to harmonize with each other. Additionally, a court should avoid an interpretation of a contract that renders portions of the language of the contract meaningless.[44]

"[I]t is a cardinal rule of contract construction that a court should, if possible, construe a contract so as not to render

---

[39]   *Transportation Ins. Co., v. Piedmont Const. Group, LLC*, 301 Ga. App. 17, 22, 686 S.E.2d 824, 829 (2009).

[40]   *Hurst v. Grange Mut. Cas. Co.*, 266 Ga. 712, 716, 470 S.E.2d 659, 663 (1996).

[41]   *Cole v. Life Ins. Co. of Georgia*, 236 Ga. App. 229, 229, 511 S.E.2d 596, 597 (1999) (reversing trial court that erred "[b]y allowing the provision most favorable to the insurance company to control").

[42]   *Id.*

[43]   *Davis v. United Am. Life Ins. Co.*, 215 Ga. 521, 527, 111 S.E.2d 488, 492 (1959).

[44]   *ALEA London Ltd. v. Woodcock*, 286 Ga. App. 572, 576, 649 S.E.2d 740 (2007), citing *Southern Trust Ins. Co. v. Dr. T's Nature Products Co.*, 261 Ga. App. 806, 807, 584 S.E.2d 34 (2003), O.C.G.A. § 13-2-2(4) ("the whole contract should be looked to in arriving at the construction of any part") and *Bd. of Regents v. A.B. & E., Inc.* 182 Ga. App. 671, 675, 357 S.E.2d 100 (1987).

any of its provisions meaningless and in a manner that gives effect to all of the contractual terms." *Pomerance*, 288 Ga. App. at 494, 654 S.E.2d at 641.

A court may not construe an insurance policy in a way that renders a provision superfluous. *York Ins. Co. v. Williams Seafood of Albany, Inc.*, 273 Ga. 710, 712, 544 S.E.2d 156, 157 (2001). This Court "must consider [the policy] as a whole, give effect to each provision, and interpret each provision to harmonize with each other." *S. Trust Ins. Co. v. Dr. T's Nature Products Co.*, 261 Ga. App. 806, 807, 584 S.E.2d 34, 35-36 (2003).

As a corollary of this rule, when a contract uses two different terms in short sequence, the terms cannot have the same meaning. *Ins. Co. of Pennsylvania v. APAC-Se., Inc.*, 297 Ga. App. 553, 558-59, 677 S.E.2d 734, 739 (2009), *citing, Pomerance v. Berkshire Life Ins. Co. of Am.*, 288 Ga. App. 491, 494-95, 654 S.E.2d 638 (2007) (rejecting interpretation of the word "substantial" that would render it interchangeable with the word "material"), *and Tyson v. McPhail Properties,* 223 Ga. App. 683, 689, 478 S.E.2d 467 (1996) (concluding that contract "would not have used two different terms in two sequential paragraphs to describe the same thing").

§ 1.8   ENDORSEMENTS

An endorsement is "[a] provision added to an insurance contract whereby the scope of its coverage is restricted or enlarged."[45] The terms of an endorsement take precedence over printed portions of the policy.[46] Multiple endorsements can combine with the policy form to create ambiguities.[47]

---

[45] *Ross v. Stephens*, 269 Ga. 266, 268, 496 S.E.2d 705, 708 (1998).
[46] *Ross v. Stephens*, 269 Ga. 266, 268-69, 496 S.E.2d 705, 708 (1998).
[47] *Georgia Farm Bureau Mut. Ins. Co. v. Meyers*, 249 Ga. App. 322, 324, 548 S.E.2d 67, 69 (2001).

§ 1.9   BURDENS

The burden of proof is on the insured to show that there is a loss covered by the policy.[48] The insurer has the burden of showing that any exclusion applies.[49] The insurer may not fulfill that burden by showing an absence of evidence, but must show that the exclusion applies "without dispute."[50]

§ 1.10   READING AN INSURANCE POLICY

Although the law can guide a practitioner in interpreting the various component parts of an insurance policy, the ability to analyze a policy and render a competent coverage analysis requires certain practical considerations. An opinion regarding coverage cannot be confidently given without consideration of all of the following:

Do you have a complete and accurate copy of the policy? Few insureds ever obtain, much less maintain, a complete and accurate copy of their policies. Although a commercial broker will often maintain or be able to reconstruct a complete and accurate copy, many retail agents will, in response to a request for a copy of the policy, provide a declarations page and state-specific endorsements without all policy forms. The only way to be sure to have a complete and accurate copy is to obtain a certified copy of the policy from the insurer. A certified copy is one assembled by the insurer and attested to, under oath, as to being complete and accurate.

---

[48] *Chix v. Georgia Farm Bur. Ins. Co.*, 150 Ga. App. 453, 258 S.E.2d 208 (1979).

[49] *St. Paul Re. v. Ross*, 276 Ga. App. 135, 622 S.E.2d 374 (2005), *cert. denied*, March 27, 2006.

[50] *Hathaway Dev. Co., Inc. v. Am. Empire Surplus Lines Ins. Co.*, 301 Ga. App. 65, 70, 686 S.E.2d 855, 861 (2009) (explaining that to prevail on an exclusion, the insurer "must establish without dispute" that the exclusion applies), *cert. granted* (May 3, 2010), *aff'd*, 288 Ga. 749, 707 S.E.2d 369 (2011).

The declarations page provides individualized details about the insured, the insurer and the coverage provided. It lists the precise entity insured and sometimes additional insureds. It specifies the name of the insurer, which is the proper entity to name in any suit on the policy. A declarations page also provides the limits potentially available for each type of coverage. Entering a limit is often the method of indicating what coverages are available. The declarations page sets the amount of the deductible. Finally, a declarations page should list the forms and endorsements that make up the complete and accurate policy. Any analysis of the policy should begin with a comparison of the list of forms and endorsements with those actually attached to ensure that all forms referenced are present and that no form present is not referenced.

The coverage clause (or insuring clause or coverage grant) is the meat of the policy and the first substantive element for analysis. Many policies have multiple coverages and multiple coverage clauses. For example, most automobile policies provide property coverage for damage to the insured's vehicle and liability coverage for bodily injury or property damage the insured may cause to third parties. In the commercial context, a business might have a single "policy" providing coverage for property damage, loss of business income, general liability, employment liability, or even kidnap and ransom insurance for traveling executives. Each must be read separately, though they sometimes reference each other.

What a coverage clause giveth, an exclusion may taketh away. Each exclusion should be separately considered with respect to the attendant circumstances of each loss, bearing in mind the rule of narrow construction described *supra*.

Conditions describe the tasks and procedures the parties must follow both before and after a loss. Conditions include the familiar notice and cooperation provisions that often constitute conditions precedent to coverage. The conditions section will also contain procedures and time limits applicable to the insurer in adjusting and paying the loss. Many policies include condition sections that apply only to a particular coverage as well as a section of "general" conditions that apply to all coverages. Thus, not all conditions necessarily apply to each loss.

Most policies contain a definitions section. Definitions must be read simultaneously with the other policy components. Although purporting to merely define certain words and phrases, many definitions severely restrict or enlarge coverage.

Endorsements must be considered with a view as to how they alter the provisions previously considered. Endorsements may go so far as to add entirely new coverage sections, delete a previous endorsement, or merely define a word or phrase. When reading an endorsement that purports to alter previous language, it is helpful to actually note such deletions on the portion of the policy referenced by the endorsement.

Grants of coverage, conditions, exclusions, definitions, endorsements and even declarations pages are read in accordance with the rules of contract construction described *supra*.

CHAPTER 2

STATUTORY BAD FAITH

§ 2.1 INTRODUCTION

Generally, a mere breach of a valid contract amounting to no more than a failure to perform creates a cause of action in contract, but not in tort.[1] Thus, under the common law, an insurer's failure to pay amounts due under an insurance policy allowed an insured to recover only the amounts that would have been due under the insurance contract. An insured had no cause of action against an insurer for simple negligence in handling a first-party claim.[2] This common law created an incentive for insurance companies to delay payment and deny coverage in close cases, as the worst-case scenario for an insurer later deemed to have unnecessarily delayed payment or to have denied coverage incorrectly was to be forced to pay the amount the insurer should have paid to begin with.[3] The expense, risk and duration of litigation further incentivize nonpayment. Many insureds will abandon or compromise their claims because they do not want to pay or cannot afford to pay an attorney, cannot be guaranteed success, or likely need some funds quickly to restore damaged property.

To partly alleviate these situations, O.C.G.A. § 33-4-6 provides for additional damages when an insurance company, following a demand from the insured, persists in its refusal

---

[1] *Tate v. Aetna Cas. & Sur. Co.*, 149 Ga. App. 123, 124, 253 S.E.2d 775, 777 (1979). A failure to perform certain duties under the insurance contract can give rise to a cause of action in tort. *See*, Chapter 3, *infra*.

[2] *Arrow Exterminators, Inc. v. Zurich American Ins. Co.*, 136 F. Supp. 2d 1340, 1354-55 (N.D. Ga. 2001).

[3] This incentive arises in the insurance context more commonly than in the context of other contractual relationships. One explanation involves the order of performance by one party (the insured) and the speculative nature of performance by the other party (the insurer). Unlike the purchaser in other contractual relationships, the insured pays the amount due under the contract (the premium) in advance of any duty by the insurer for it to perform its duties under the contract.

to pay amounts due under a policy in "bad faith." Early on, Georgia courts recognized that the purpose of the statute was to remove the incentive for unnecessary delay[4] and to create a situation allowing an insured to be made whole in the event the insured is forced to go to court to enforce the insurance contract.[5] For this reason, the statute can be particularly ineffective as applied to low-value losses. For example, the statutory penalty for failure to pay a $20,000 loss is only $10,000 (50% of limits, *see*, O.C.G.A. § 33-4-6(a), set forth below). A large, for-profit carrier might not be fearful of such a penalty, knowing that the insured must hire an attorney and pay for expert witnesses and other litigation expenses with little upside for the risk undertaken.

O.C.G.A. § 33-4-6(a) states as follows:

> In the event of a loss which is covered by a policy of insurance and the refusal of the insurer to pay the same within 60 days after a demand has been made by the holder of the policy and a finding has been made that such refusal was in bad faith, the insurer shall be liable to pay such holder, in addition to the loss, not more than 50 percent of the liability of the insurer for the loss or $5,000.00, whichever is greater, and all reasonable attorney's fees for the prosecution of the action against the insurer. The action for bad faith shall not be abated by payment after the 60 day period nor shall the testimony or opinion of an expert witness be the sole basis for a summary judgment or directed verdict on the issue of bad faith. The amount of any reasonable attorney's fees shall be determined by the trial jury and shall be included in any judg-

---

[4] "The purpose of the law was evidently to force prompt payment of such losses, after the lapse of a reasonable time." *Cotton States Life Ins. Co. v. Edwards*, 74 Ga. 220, 1884 WL 2537, *8.

[5] "The [statutory bad-faith penalty] is one of the inherent rights attaching to a contract of insurance to enable the beneficiaries to obtain, free from deduction, the original benefits of the provision in their favor, according to the tenor of the policy." *Metropolitan Life Ins. Co. v. Lathan*, 77 Ga. App. 6, 11, 47 S.E.2d 596, 597 (1948).

ment which is rendered in the action; provided, however, the attorney's fees shall be fixed on the basis of competent expert evidence as to the reasonable value of the services based on the time spent and legal and factual issues involved in accordance with prevailing fees in the locality where the action is pending; provided, further, the trial court shall have the discretion, if it finds the jury verdict fixing attorney's fees to be greatly excessive or inadequate, to review and amend the portion of the verdict fixing attorney's fees without the necessity of disapproving the entire verdict. The limitations contained in this Code section in reference to the amount of attorney's fees are not controlling as to the fees which may be agreed upon by the plaintiff and the plaintiff's attorney for the services of the attorney in the action against the insurer.

Many courts have held that because the statute imposes a penalty, its requirements are strictly construed.[6] To prevail on a claim for an insurer's bad faith under O.C.G.A. § 33-4-6, the insured must show that (1) the claim is covered under the policy; (2) a demand for payment was made against the insurer 60 days prior to filing suit; and (3) the insurer's refusal to pay was in bad faith.[7]

The statute also requires that the insured plaintiff "mail to the Commissioner of Insurance and the consumers' insurance advocate a copy of the demand and complaint by first-class mail."[8] Ironically, Georgia has no official with the title of "consumers' insurance advocate." The office of the Commissioner of Insurance is aware of the statutory requirement and the impossibility of literal compliance. Practition-

---

[6] *E.g., Interstate Life & Acc. Ins. Co. v. Williamson*, 220 Ga. 323, 325, 138 S.E.2d 668, 669 (1964) ("The recovery provided in the [bad-faith statute], is a penalty. Penalties and forfeitures are not favored. The right to such recovery must be clearly shown.").

[7] *Lavoi Corp. v. National Fire Ins. Co. of Hartford*, 293 Ga. App. 142, 146, 666 S.E.2d 387 (2008), *citing* O.C.G.A. § 33-4-6.

[8] O.C.G.A. § 33-4-6(b).

ers may mail the complaint and demand to the office of the commissioner, who, in the authors' experience, promptly sends written confirmation of receipt, helpfully reciting compliance with the statute.[9]

§ 2.2   FAILURE TO PAY A COVERED "LOSS"

The statute opens with the requirement that there be a "loss" covered by a policy. Thus, the insured must prove that the loss for which payment sought is covered under the insurance policy at issue. Where the claim is not covered, the insurer has no obligation to pay and there can be no bad faith.[10]

The vast majority of cases applying O.C.G.A. § 33-4-6 involve the insurance company's failure to pay a loss under "first-party" coverage. First-party coverage includes claims involving only the insured and the insurer, such as payment for property damage to a home following a fire or the payment of benefits under a life or disability policy.[11] An increasing number of statutory bad faith cases, however, in-

---

[9]   The authors send a file-stamped copy of the complaint and the demand addressed as follows: Commissioner of Insurance, Consumers' Insurance Advocate, 716 West Tower, Two MLK Jr. Drive, Atlanta, GA 30334. Although failure to comply may be cured, O.C.G.A. § 33-4-6(b), the recommended practice is to comply immediately upon filing the complaint. The letter to the commissioner and the commissioner's letter confirming receipt should then be produced in the early stages of discovery.

[10]   See Collins v. Life Ins. Co. of Georgia, 228 Ga. App. 301, 303, 491 S.E.2d 514 (1997) (even where insurer was alleged to have misrepresented whether a "prosthesis" was covered under the policy, award for bad-faith refusal to pay was not authorized because the contract did not cover "prosthesis" and the insurer cannot be deemed to have acted in bad faith for a refusal to pay what is clearly not covered); Rich v. Georgia Farm Bureau Mut. Ins. Co., 176 Ga. App. 663, 663, 337 S.E.2d 370 (1985) (insurer not liable for refusal to pay for property that was damaged but was not covered under policy).

[11]   The insurance industry distinguishes between "first-party" and "third-party" claims. The "first party" is the insured who has a claim for payment as a direct beneficiary under an insurance policy. A first-party claim generally involves only the insurer and the insured. A "third party" is a claimant who is not a party to the insurance contract but has a claim against an insured who might be covered under a liability policy. Thus, a third-party claim involves three parties: the insurer, the insured and the third-party claimant.

volve the insurance company's failure to provide coverage or a defense under a "third-party" liability policy.[12] An earlier and instructive example is *Leader Nat. Ins. Co. v. Kemp & Son, Inc.*[13] In that case, the insurer failed to defend an insured under a liability policy, leading to judgments against the insured in excess of policy limits. The insured sued the insurer. At trial, the jury awarded the amount of the excess judgments, post-judgment interest and the statutory penalty, which at the time was twenty-five percent. Both the Court of Appeals and the Supreme Court of Georgia affirmed. The authors predict Georgia law to further develop in the coming years with respect to the relevance of O.C.G.A. § 33-4-6 in claims involving the alleged breach of a third-party liability policy. Any such development must focus on the meaning of "loss" in the statute.

At present, there is a "loss" within the meaning of O.C.G.A. § 33-4-6 and bad faith damages are possible in cases involving a breach of the duty to defend under a liability policy.[14] In *Transportation Ins. Co. v. Piedmont Construction Group, LLC*,[15] the insured was a contractor whose subcontractor caused a fire to the owner's building. The owner sued the contractor, who tendered the case to its liability insurer. The insurer refused to defend the contractor. The insured provided its own defense and filed an action against its insurer. The court held that the insurer breached the duty to defend in bad faith, and that the attorneys' fees incurred by the insured in its own defense was a "loss" within the meaning of O.C.G.A. § 33-4-6(a).[16] The court did not specifically

---

[12] Physical precedence, but not much guidance, may be found in *OneBeacon Am. Ins. Co. v. Catholic Diocese of Savannah*, 2011 WL 3878337 (S.D. Ga. 2011) and *Landmark Am. Ins. Co. v. Khan*, 307 Ga. App. 609, 705 S.E.2d 707 (2011), *cert. denied* (Sept. 6, 2011).

[13] 189 Ga. App. 115, 375 S.E.2d 231 (1988) *aff'd*, 259 Ga. 329, 380 S.E.2d 458 (1989).

[14] *Federal Ins. Co. v. National Distributing Co., Inc.*, 203 Ga. App. 763, 417 S.E.2d 671 (1992) (finding no bad faith on other grounds).

[15] 301 Ga. App. 17, 26, 686 S.E.2d 824 (2009), *cert denied*, March 29, 2010.

[16] *Id.* 301 Ga. App. at 26, 686 S.E.2d 824.

address whether any amounts the insurer failed to pay in indemnification of a judgment constituted a "loss" under the statute.

§ 2.3   TIMELY DEMAND

A proper "demand" for payment that complies with O.C.G.A. § 33-4-6 is essential to recovery.[17] In evaluating the sufficiency of a demand, a court should consider its purpose.[18] The purpose of the demand requirement "is to adequately notify an insurer that it is facing a bad faith claim so that it may make a decision about whether to pay, deny or further investigate the claim within the 60-day deadline."[19]

On its face, the demand requirement is straightforward. The statute's plain language would appear to require only that the insurer refuse to pay within 60 days of a demand. This straightforward language notwithstanding, courts have added additional requirements to the demand through case law. Because of the case law, no element of statutory bad faith provides more opportunity for the insured to forfeit an otherwise valid cause of action for bad faith than a failure to meet the deceptively simple demand requirement. In summary, Georgia courts and courts applying Georgia law have interpreted the statute to require that a demand (a) be sent to the insurer 60 days prior to filing a lawsuit; (b) be sent at a time the loss is due and payable; (c) include (in some cases) a threat of litigation; and (d) reference a specific loss.[20]

---

[17] *Cagle v. State Farm Fire & Cas Co.*, 236 Ga. App. 726, 727, 512 S.E.2d 717 (1999).

[18] *Primerica Life Ins. Co. v. Humfleet*, 217 Ga. App. 770, 772, 458 S.E.2d 908 (1995).

[19] *Id.*

[20] This attempt to list the "elements" of a statutory bad-faith notice is the result of the authors' experience in such cases and a reading of the reported cases. This specific list appears nowhere in the case law of which the authors are aware.

    (a)   Demand must be prior to lawsuit.

The literal language of the statute states that there must be a "refusal of the insurer to pay the [loss] within 60 days after a demand has been made." This language would not appear to foreclose the filing of a bad-faith lawsuit prior to 60 days after the demand has been made if the insurer were to issue a written, unequivocal refusal to pay following its receipt of the demand but prior to 60 days having run. Such a reading would be consistent with the notion that the demand be sent such that the insurer has at least 60 days to decide whether to pay the claim or refuse to pay the claim before the lawsuit is filed.[21] Nonetheless, other courts have expressed the requirement more strictly, writing that "a failure to wait at least 60 days between making demand and filing suit constitutes an absolute bar to recovery of a bad-faith penalty and attorney fees under this statute."[22] Until there is more clarity on this issue, the conservative approach would counsel waiting 60 days after the demand to file the suit, an intervening refusal to pay notwithstanding.

    (b)   Immediate payment due.

To be timely, a demand for payment may not be made before immediate payment is in order.[23] In *Cagle v. State Farm Fire & Cas Co.*, the policy stated that a loss was not payable until 60 days after the insured submitted a proof of loss.[24] The insured had submitted a proof of loss approximately 55 days before filing the lawsuit.[25] The court stated that the demand did not appear to be proper, because the insured was not entitled to immediate payment until 60 days after it had submitted a proof of loss.

---

[21] *Cagle v. State Farm Fire & Cas Co.*, 236 Ga. App. 726, 726, 512 S.E.2d 717 (1999).

[22] *Blue Cross & Blue Shield v. Merrell*, 170 Ga. App. 86, 87, 316 S.E.2d 548 (1984).

[23] *Cagle v. State Farm Fire and Casualty Co.*, 236 Ga. App. 726, 512 S.E.2d 717 (1999), *cert. denied*, June 3, 1999.

[24] *Id.*

[25] *Id.* 236 Ga. App. at 728, 512 S.E.2d 717, n. 2.

An insured is not in a position to demand immediate payment, and a demand is premature, if the insurer has additional time left under the terms of the insurance policy in which to investigate or adjust the loss.[26] In *Dixie Construction Products Inc. v. WMH Inc.*, the insured claimed it had made sufficient demand by May 4.[27] The insured's agent testified that he had submitted the final figures for adjustment of the claim on May 10. The agent further stated that he figured the adjuster would need a reasonable amount of time to process the final figures and other claim information following its submission.[28] The trial court found the demand to be premature as a matter of law. The Court of Appeals affirmed, holding that there was no evidence that the insured was legally in a position to demand immediate payment more than 60 days before it filed the lawsuit.[29]

Similarly, if the policyholder submits additional information after having sent a demand, and the insurer needed the information to determine whether the claim was payable, bad faith may be defeated as a matter of law.[30] In *Balboa Life and Cas., LLC v. Home Builders Finance, Inc.*, a mortgagee was a loss payee under a property policy. The mortgagee sent a demand letter to the insurer. The insurer responded with a request for "information relevant to determine the mortgagee's interest in the insurance proceeds."[31] The mortgagee filed a bad-faith lawsuit less than 60 days later, defeating the bad-faith claim as a matter of law.

If an insurance policy states that the insurer does not have to pay until 30 days after receipt of a proof of loss, a demand is untimely if made before 30 days after the proof of loss is

---

[26] *Dixie Construction Products Inc. v. WMH Inc.*, 179 Ga. App. 658, 347 S.E.2d 303 (1986).

[27] *Id.*

[28] *Id.*

[29] *Id.*

[30] *Balboa Life and Cas., LLC v. Home Builders Finance, Inc.*, 304 Ga. App. 478, 697 S.E. 2d 240 (2010).

[31] *Balboa Life & Cas., LLC v. Home Builders Fin., Inc.*, 304 Ga. App. 478, 483, 697 S.E.2d 240, 245 (2010).

submitted.[32] An insurer may waive the requirement to file a proof of loss form.[33]

(c)   Specter or threat of litigation.

O.C.G.A. § 33-4-6 requires no specific content of the demand, and the plain language includes no requirement that the insured threaten litigation or a bad-faith lawsuit. Despite the lack of such a requirement, some courts have required that "the language used must be sufficient to alert the insurer that it is facing a bad faith claim for a specific refusal to pay so that it may decide whether to pay the claim."[34] As explained below, the case law reflects a subtle distinction in regard to the level of threat necessary.

On one end of the spectrum, some courts have required that the demand reflect only "the mere specter of a lawsuit."[35] In *Southern Realty Mgmt., Inc. v. Aspen Specialty Ins. Co.*, the insured's attorney sent a letter to the insurer demanding payment of the amounts included in the proofs of loss submitted four months earlier and stating, "This letter is a formal demand for payment under the referenced policies and applicable law, and should be considered a demand for payment under the provisions of the Georgia Code pertaining to a refusal by an insurer to pay an insured's loss after demand." Although the letter did not specifically threaten litigation or cite to the statute, it was a sufficient demand.[36]

---

[32]   *Lavoi Corp. v. National Fire Ins. Co. of Hartford*, 293 Ga. App. 142, 146, 666 S.E.2d 387 (2008).

[33]   *Buffalo Ins. Co. v. Star Photofinishing Co.*, 120 Ga. App. 697, 702, 172 S.E.2d 159 (1969); *Britt v. Independent Fire Ins. Co.*, 184 Ga. App. 225, 227, 361 S.E.2d 226 (1987) and O.C.G.A. § 33-24-39 (requiring insurer to furnish a proof of loss form and stating that the failure to furnish the form "upon request or written notice of a loss shall constitute waiver of the right of the insurer to require proof of loss").

[34]   *Bayrock Mortg. Corp. v. Chicago Title Ins. Co.*, 286 Ga. App. 18, 20, 648 S.E.2d 433, 435 (2007).

[35]   *Southern Realty Mgmt., Inc. v. Aspen Specialty Ins. Co.*, 2008 WL 4787511 (N.D. Ga. 2008).

[36]   Barely. The court scolded the insured for not having more clearly invoked the statute, writing as follows: "The present difficulty might have been

Because the statute addresses solely litigation between insurers and insureds, it is logical to assume that including a citation to the statute (though not required by the plain terms of the statute) puts an insurer on notice of possible litigation.

A more recent case examined two letters from the insured and determined that in combination the "transactions constituted a demand" under the statute.[37] In *Byce v. Pruco Life Ins. Co.*, the insured's first letter stated that "I respectfully request immediate payment." The court ruled that "respectful language does not overcome the clear intent of the letter which was to demand payment." The court further ruled, however, that because the letter did not use the phrase "bad faith" or cite to the statute "as a shorthand," the first letter did not "on its own" constitute a proper demand. The second letter did not "actually state that [the insured] will sue," but it did state that the insured did not "waive her right to sue [the insurer] at any time for its bad faith refusal to pay."[38] The court ruled that "[t]hese letters taken together clearly indicate that, at a minimum, 'a mere specter' of a bad faith lawsuit existed." Thus, the two letters constituted a "transaction" that in turn constituted proper demand.

On the other end of the spectrum, several courts have dismissed bad-faith claims for the failure of the demand to sufficiently threaten bad-faith litigation.[39] For example, a letter to the insurer from the insured's attorney that complains of "stonewalling," refers to "unacceptable" and "negligent" adjusting practices and promises to "hold [the insurer] fully responsible" for any failure to pay was held to be insufficient

---

avoided had counsel simply invoked the statute or used the words "bad faith." *S. Realty Mgmt., Inc. v. Aspen Specialty Ins. Co.*, 2008 WL 4787511, *3 (N.D. Ga.).

[37] *Byce v. Pruco Life Ins. Co.*, 2011 WL 233390 (N.D. Ga. 2011).

[38] *Id.*, citing *Mut. Sav. Life Ins. Co. v. Hines*, 96 Ga. App. 442, 449, 100 S.E.2d 466, 472 (1957).

[39] The requirement that litigation be threatened (by way of citation to the statute or more directly) is arguably a judge-made requirement with no statutory support. Nonetheless, based on the case law, a practitioner ignores the requirement at the peril of forfeiting the cause of action.

as a matter of law.[40] In *Arrow Exterminators, Inc. v. Zurich American Ins. Co.*, the court faulted the letter for failing to reference a claim for "bad faith," failing to cite to the statute as a "shorthand" reference or failing to state that the insured was contemplating litigation.[41] Because of these failures, the insurer was not on sufficient notice that it had 60 days to make a decision or face possible penalties, and the bad-faith claim was dismissed.

The above requirements notwithstanding, a demand may be oral.[42] In *Clark*, the insured stated to an adjuster "[w]ell, if you won't pay me I will have to take you in [sic] court," and the adjuster responded, "I'll see you in court."[43] Significantly, the demand was oral and did not reference the penalty available under the statute. Nonetheless, this exchange constituted a sufficient demand under O.C.G.A. § 33-4-6(a).[44] Although such an oral demand presents a flare for the dramatic, written demands continue to be the safer practice and provide the clearer proof that the demand was properly made.

Mere submission of a proof of loss is not a "demand" for payment, nor is the mere submission of bills.[45]

---

[40] *Arrow Exterminators, Inc. v. Zurich American Ins. Co.*, 136 F. Supp. 2d 1340, 1356-57 (N.D. Ga. 2001).

[41] *Id.*

[42] *Cotton States Mut. Ins. Co. v. Clark*, 114 Ga. App. 439, 447, 151 S.E.2d 780 (1966).

[43] *Id.* 114 Ga. App. at 447, 151 S.E.2d 780 (1966).

[44] *Id.*

[45] *Brown v. Ohio Casualty Ins. Co.*, 239 Ga. App. 251, 519 S.E.2d 726 (1999) (claimant submitted proof of loss but failed to make any demand for payment prior to filing suit); *Blue Cross & Blue Shield of Georgia/Atlanta, Inc. v. Merrell*, 170 Ga. App. 86, 316 S.E.2d 548 (1984) (claimant claimed to have submitted medical bills to insurer, but there was no evidence in the record that she had done so – rather, she filed her complaint without any prior demand); *Guarantee Life Ins. Co. v. Norris*, 219 Ga. 573, 134 S.E.2d 774 (1964) (claimant submitted a proof of loss but did not demand payment).

(d)   Specific loss.

A notice that fails to demand payment for a specific loss is insufficient.[46] *Arrow Exterminators, Inc. v. Zurich American Ins. Co.* is again instructive, because the letter merely expressed general dissatisfaction with the manner in which the insurer adjusted a series of claims rather than demanding payment for a specific claim.[47] The failure to demand payment in a particular sum, however, does not necessarily render the demand insufficient.[48] Indeed, the mere fact that a jury awards only 59 percent of the damages sought in a demand does not defeat bad faith as a matter of law.[49]

Where an insurer files a declaratory judgment to determine its contractual duty to the insured, the insurer waives the 60-day notice requirement of O.C.G.A. § 33-4-6.[50]

PRACTICE POINTER: Ideally, a demand should be sent after the insurance company has formally denied coverage, removing most potential objections as to whether the demand prematurely interrupted the claims-adjusting process. When possible, a practitioner should attempt to review the entire insurance policy and make sure conditions precedent and other duties of the insured have been satisfied before sending a formal demand. A formal, written demand is preferred over an oral demand for reasons of proof. Some practitioners put something like the following legend across the top of the demand letter: BAD-FAITH DEMAND FOR IMMEDIATE PAYMENT UNDER O.C.G.A. § 33-4-6. Some also include in the letter a sentence like the following: "In the event that [insurance company] fails to pay all amounts due

---

[46] *Arrow Exterminators, Inc. v. Zurich American Ins. Co.*, 136 F. Supp. 2d 1340, 1357 (N.D. Ga. 2001).

[47] *Id.* 136 F. Supp. 2d at 1357.

[48] *Hanover Ins. Co. v. Hallford*, 127 Ga. App. 322, 324, 193 S.E.2d 235 (1972).

[49] *Hendley v. Am. Nat'l Fire Ins. Co.*, 842 F. 2d 267, 268 (11th Cir. 1988).

[50] *Leader National Ins. Co. v. Kemp*, 189 Ga. App. 115, 118, 375 S.E.2d 231 (1988), *aff'd*, 259 Ga. 329, 380 S.E.2d 458 (1989).

within the time provided for in O.C.G.A. § 33-4-6, [insured] will file a lawsuit against [insurance company] seeking all amounts due under the policy as well as the penalty and attorney's fees provided for in O.C.G.A. § 33-4-6."

§ 2.4   BAD-FAITH FAILURE TO PAY

The insured has the burden of showing that an insurer's refusal to pay a claim was in bad faith.[51] The question of bad faith is for the trier of fact,[52] and the existence vel non of bad faith is a jury question.[53] A finding that the insurance company failed to pay a valid claim and breached the insurance policy does not necessarily constitute bad faith by itself nor does it set up a presumption as to bad faith.[54] Rather, actual "bad faith" must be shown. Georgia courts have stated the test for bad faith in various ways over the years:

(1) Some courts have referred to a lack of "reasonable and probable cause" for failing to pay the claim: "The Georgia test for bad faith is whether the insurer had 'reasonable and

---

[51] *Interstate Life & Acc. Ins. Co. v. Williamson*, 220 Ga. 323, 324, 138 S.E.2d 668 (1964) (answering certified question); *Atlantic Title Ins. Co. v. Aegis Funding Corp.*, 287 Ga. App. 392, 393, 651 S.E. 2d 507, 508 (2007) ("To support a cause of action under [Georgia's Bad Faith Statute], the insured bears the burden of proving that the refusal to pay the claim was made in bad faith."), *cert. denied*, Jan. 28, 2008.

[52] *First Financial Ins. Co. v. Am. Sandblasting Co.*, 223 Ga. App. 232, 477 S.E. 2d 390, 392 (1996); *Colonial Life & Accident Ins. Co. v. McLain*, 243 Ga. 263, 265, 253 S.E. 2d 745, 746 (1979) ("Not every defense bars a finding of bad faith. It is a defense which raises a reasonable question of law or a reasonable issue of fact even though not accepted by the trial court or jury."); *Interstate Life & Accident Ins. Co. v. Williamson*, 220 Ga. 323, 325, 138 S.E.2d 668 (1964) ("The [bad] faith of the company should not be judged by the preliminary proofs, or other ex parte affidavits, but by the case made at the trial.").

[53] *Selective Way Ins. Co. v. Litigation Technology Inc.*, 270 Ga. App. 38, 41, 606 S.E. 2d 68, 71-72 (2004), *cert. denied*, Jan. 24 2005.

[54] *Florida Internat'l Indem. Co. v. Osgood*, 233 Ga. App. 111, 116, 503 S.E. 2d 371, 376 (1998) (finding no bad faith as a matter of law even though claim was payable); and *Winningham v. Centennial Ins. Co.*, 708 F.2d 658, 659 (11th Cir. 1983) (noting that bad-faith damages are "not automatically imposed on an insurance company every time it refuses to pay the underlying claim prior to trial and the insured successfully litigates the dispute").

probable cause' for defending against the claim."[55]   The Court of Appeals similarly stated recently that "[t]he insurer's defense to the coverage must be reasonable under the circumstances presented in the case."[56]

(2)   Similarly, other courts have looked to the absence of "good cause" for failing to pay the claim: "Bad faith is shown by evidence that under the terms of the policy under which the demand is made and under the facts surrounding the response to that demand, the insurer had no 'good cause' for resisting and delaying payment."[57]

(3)   Finally, other courts have stated that the refusal to pay the claim must be for some "frivolous or unfounded" reason: "Bad faith, as that term is defined in [O.C.G.A. § 33-4-6] means any frivolous and unfounded refusal in law or in fact to comply with the demand of the policyholder to pay according to the terms of the policy."[58]

(The standard for statutory bad faith should not be confused with the standard applicable in a case alleging bad faith failure to settle a liability claim, which is governed by the common law.[59])

---

[55] *Winningham v. Centennial Ins. Co.*, 708 F.2d 658, 659 (11th Cir. 1983). "A defense going far enough to show reasonable and probable cause for making it, would vindicate the good faith of the company as effectually as would a complete defense to the action." *Fountain v. Unum Life Ins. Co. of Am.*, 297 Ga. App. 458, 462, 677 S.E. 2d 334, 338 (2009) (finding no bad faith as a matter of law because insurer had reasonable grounds for disputing whether insured was "totally disabled" within meaning of disability policy).

[56] *Lloyd's Syndicate No. 5820 v. AGCO Corp.*, ___ Ga. App. ___, 734 S.E.2d 899, 904 (2012) (denying summary judgment to insurer on bad faith because the court could not conclude that "the refusal to pay was reasonable as a matter of law").

[57] *Lawyers Title Ins. Corp. v. Griffin*, 302 Ga. App. 726, 731, 691 S.E.2d 633, 637 (2010) (emphasis in original).

[58] *Interstate Life & Acc. Ins. Co. v. Williamson*, 220 Ga. 323, 324-25, 138 S.E.2d 668 (1964), *citing* Royal Ins. Co. Ltd. v. Cohen, 105 Ga. App. 746, 747, 125 S.E.2d 709 (1962) and *American Fire & Cas. Co. v. Barfield*, 81 Ga. App. 887, 887, 60 S.E.2d 383 (1950).

[59] *See* Chapter 3, *infra.*

On their face, the standards may be seen as different sides of the same coin. Indeed, many courts use language from all three standards in the same decision. Arguably, the "reasonable and probable cause" and "no good cause" standards are advantageous to the insured while the "frivolous and unfounded" standard is advantageous to the insurance company. This is because finding that a defense for nonpayment lacks "good cause" suggests that the insurance company's defense may have been rejected by the court or jury only after at least some consideration of its merit. Finding that a defense for nonpayment was "frivolous or unfounded," on the other hand, suggests (if the words are taken to their extreme) that the defense clearly lacked merit on its face, needing little or no consideration whatsoever. Accordingly, an insurer will often argue application of the "frivolous or unfounded" standard, while the insured will argue application of the "no good cause" standard. Both will find support for their respective arguments, as both standards appear in the case law.

The appearance of both standards in the case law notwithstanding, the "no good cause" standard better represents the modern view. Computer-assisted legal research reveals more than 100 cases using the terms "insurance," "bad faith," "frivolous" and "unfounded." Far fewer occur when the phrase "good cause" replaces the terms "frivolous" and "unfounded" in the same search. The dates on the reported cases, however, are revealing. The "frivolous or unfounded" standard appears as early as 1884.[60] The "good cause" standard has not been consistently applied until more recently, but its appearance in the very latest cases suggests its increasing prevalence.[61]

---

[60] *Cotton States Life Ins. Co. v. Edwards*, 74 Ga. 220, 1884 WL 2537, *8 (describing bad faith as "any frivolous or unfounded refusal in law or in fact to comply with the requisition of the policy-holder to pay according to the terms of his contract and the conditions imposed by statute").

[61] *Jimenez v. Chicago Title Ins. Co.*, 310 Ga. App. 9, 12, 712 S.E.2d 531, 535 (2011) ("Bad faith may be shown by demonstrating that under the policy "and under the facts surrounding the response to that demand, the insurer had no

No matter the fine distinctions or parsing the terms used, acquiring an understanding of what constitutes bad faith is best done by reading case law. Accordingly, several illustrative examples are provided below.

(a)   Bad faith and ambiguous policy provisions.

Most bad-faith cases involve disagreements over the meaning of a particular provision of the insurance policy, the resolution of which resolves the issue of coverage. Where the insured prevails on the coverage issue in such cases, it will sometimes be because the court found the provision ambiguous and construed it in favor of coverage.[62] Notwithstanding a ruling in favor of coverage in a particular case, the issue of whether the insurance company relied on the ambiguous provision in "bad faith" would still remain. The cases are mixed as to whether an insurer can face liability for bad faith when the insurer denies coverage in reliance on an ambiguous policy provision. As shown below, however, the modern trend appears to be that an insurance company's reliance on an ambiguous provision does not shield the insurer from bad faith as a matter of law.

One of the earliest bad-faith cases involved ambiguity in an insurance policy. In *The Northwestern Mut. Life Ins. Co. v. Ross*,[63] the Supreme Court of Georgia found that the insurance company had relied on an ambiguous policy in denying coverage. Construing the ambiguity in favor of the insured, the Court found that coverage existed and affirmed the verdict in favor of the insured. In discussing its conclusion as

---

'good cause' for resisting and delaying payment."); *Balboa Life and Cas., LLC v. Home Builders Finanace, Inc.*, 304 Ga. App. 478, 697 S.E. 2d 240 (June, 10, 2010) ("Bad faith is shown [under OCGA § 33-4-6(a)] by evidence that under the terms of the policy upon which the demand is made and under the facts surrounding the response to that demand, the insurer had no good cause for resisting and delaying payment."); *Lawyers Title Ins. Corp. v. Griffin*, 302 Ga. App. 726, 731, 691 S.E.2d 633, 637 (2010) (same); *Atlantic Title Ins. Co. v. Aegis Funding Corp.*, 287 Ga. App. 392, 651 S.E. 2d 507 (2007) (same), *cert. denied*, Jan. 28, 2008.

[62]   *See* § 1.6, supra.

[63]   63 Ga. 199, 1879 WL 2478.

to the meaning of the operative clause, the Court referred to the fact that other jurisdictions had reached an opposite conclusion as to the meaning of the operative clause.

Turning to the issue of bad faith, the Court ruled that there could be no bad faith as a matter of law. "Where the highest courts of the country have differed in respect to the construction of a contract, and, in this state, the principle, though hinted at, had never been settled, it cannot be that to test the question here is in bad faith."[64] Thus, the court reasoned that the insurer could not be penalized for litigating its interpretation of the policy in that particular case, even though the insurer did not prevail.

A more recent case reached a different result. In *Georgia Farm Bureau v. Jackson*,[65] the named insured owned a Geo and a Taurus that were insured under two separate policies. The policy on the Geo had an accidental death benefit, which stated as follows:

> The Company will pay insured's injury coverage benefits for: ... (b) "accidental death benefit" incurred with respect to "bodily injury" sustained by an "eligible injured person" caused by an accident.... When used in reference to this coverage "accidental death benefit" means death resulting directly and independently of all other causes from "bodily injury" caused by accident while "occupying" or being struck by a "motor vehicle."

---

[64] *Id.* at *6 (emphasis in original). *See also United States Fidelity & Guar. Co. v. Woodward*, 118 Ga. App. 591, 594, 164 S.E. 2d 878, 881 (1968) (finding ambiguity, construing it in favor of coverage, but ruling that because of the "close question as to interpretation of the policy" there could be no bad faith as a matter of law). Significantly, in ruling that reliance on an ambiguous provision defeats bad faith as a matter of law, the court in *United States Fidelity & Guar. Co. v. Woodward* relied on the standard of review rejected 11 years later by the Supreme Court of Georgia in *Colonial Life & Accident Ins. Co. v. McClain*, 243 Ga. 263, 253 S.E.2d 745 (1979).

[65] 240 Ga. App. 127, 522 S.E.2d 716 (1999).

The 16-year-old daughter of the named insured was killed in an accident while driving the Taurus. The named insured made a claim under the Geo policy for the accidental death benefit, and the insurer denied the claim. The trial court granted summary judgment and bad faith penalties against the insurer.

With regard to coverage, the insurer argued on appeal that to qualify for the accidental death benefit an insured must be "struck by a motor vehicle" while a pedestrian. In rejecting the argument, the Court of Appeals relied on the general rule that policies are to be read according to the reasonable expectations of the insured and found that the language of the endorsement was not specifically tailored to apply only to pedestrians. Accordingly, the court found the language ambiguous and construed it in favor of coverage.

With regard to bad faith, the court acknowledged that an insurer is not liable for bad faith penalties where there is a doubtful question of law, but ruled that the policy was ambiguous without a doubt. The assertion that there was a "doubtful question" was based on an "implication" gathered from the policy, the court reasoned, not on specific language or doubtful facts. Accordingly, the court affirmed the trial court's finding of bad faith as a matter of law.

In another case, the court ruled that although the insurer's reliance on an ambiguous provision was "plausible," bad faith should still go to the jury.[66]

    (b)   Bad faith and the reasonableness of the insurer's interpretation of policy language.

In *Transportation Ins. Co. v. Piedmont Construction Group, LLC*,[67] the court determined that the insurance company's

---

[66] *See also First Financial Ins. Co. v. Am. Sandblasting Co.*, 223 Ga. App. 232, 477 S.E. 2d 390 (1996).

[67] 301 Ga. App. 17, 686 S.E.2d 824 (2009).

denial of coverage was based on a frivolous and unsubstantiated interpretation of policy language and the law, supporting bad faith as a matter of law. In *Transportation Ins. Co. v. Piedmont Construction Group, LLC*, the insured was a contractor renovating part of a building. A subcontractor started a fire that caused substantial damage to the entire building. The building owner sued the contractor, and the contractor sought coverage and a defense from its liability insurer. The insurer denied, relying on the so-called "business risks" exclusions, one of which bars coverage for damage to "[t]hat particular part of real property on which you or any contractors or subcontractors . . . are performing operations." The insurer relied solely on one decision of the Georgia Court of Appeals that had applied the exclusion when the insured sought liability coverage solely for its own work. In the case at bar, however, the fire had damaged parts of the owner's property that were clearly not the insured's work and not the "particular part" of the property on which the insured was working. The insurer ignored case law making the distinction clear, supporting the appellate court's decision to affirm the trial court's finding of bad faith as a matter of law.

An "unfounded" interpretation of policy language may also create a jury issue as to bad faith.[68] In *Selective Way Ins. Co. v. Litigation Technology Inc.*, the court affirmed a trial court's denial of an insurance company's motion for summary judgment on bad faith. "[The unfounded interpretation] coupled with the fact that [the insurance company] initially agreed to pay and did not assert its exclusionary defense for over a year and a half creates a jury issue as to whether it exercised bad faith in refusing to pay [the insured's] claim."[69]

---

[68] *Selective Way Ins. Co. v. Litigation Technology Inc.*, 270 Ga. App. 38, 606 S.E. 2d 68 (2004), *cert. denied*, Jan. 24 2005.

[69] *Id.* at 41, 71.

(c)   Bad faith and the reasonableness of the insurance company's factual position.

An insurer's defense "going far enough to show reasonable and probable cause for making it" vindicates the good faith of the insurer and precludes a finding of bad faith.[70] The facts must, however, be "in genuine conflict" for the insurance company to be released from bad faith as a matter of law.[71] Indeed, when faced with conflicting facts, the court's duty is to "carefully scrutinize" those facts to preclude the insurance company from relying on "fanciful allegations of factual conflict to delay or avoid legitimate claims payment."[72]

In *Cincinnati Ins. Co. v. Kastner*,[73] the insureds filed suit to recover benefits under their homeowner's policy following a burglary. The insurer's refusal to pay was based, in part, on the fact that there had been no forced entry and that the insureds' accounts of the missing items and of the location of the keys to the deadbolt doors were somewhat inconsistent. However, the inconsistencies in the insured's stories were minor, and there was ample evidence tending to point to a burglary (access from the townhouse next door was relatively easy, the insureds' neighbor had seen a stranger in the courtyard of the townhouse on the afternoon of the burglary, the townhouse was for sale and various people, including the movers, had recently been allowed access to the house). There was no evidence that the insureds had facilitated or staged the burglary nor evidence that the insureds were in possession of the items they claimed had been stolen. Thus, the insurer's rationale for its denial supported a claim for

---

[70] *Cincinnati Ins. Co. v. Kastner*, 233 Ga. App. 594, 504 S.E.2d 496 (1998), *citing Southern Fire & Cas. Ins. Co. v. Northwest Ga. Bank*, 209 Ga. App. 867, 434 S.E.2d 729 (1993).

[71] *Id.*, *citing Rice v. State Farm Fire & Cas. Co.*, 208 Ga. App. 166, 169, 430 S.E.2d 75 (1993).

[72] *Id.*

[73] 233 Ga. App. 594, 504 S.E.2d 496 (1998).

bad faith in the trial court, and the Court of Appeals affirmed the award of bad-faith damages.

Where the insurance company's investigation reasonably indicates that the insured's loss may have lead to no monetary damages whatsoever, there is no bad faith as a matter of law.[74] *Lawyers Title Ins. Corp. v. Griffin* involved a title insurance policy. The insured made a claim for a loss of an easement insured under the policy and the insurer denied coverage, arguing that the easement had no monetary value. Although the insurance company's factual position was rejected by the trier of fact, the court ruled that there was sufficient evidence of the insurer's factual position (though ultimately rejected) to defeat bad faith as a matter of law. A factual dispute, however, "must be reasonable under the circumstances presented in the case."[75]

> (d)   No bad faith where insurer has a reasonable ground to contest the claim, even though the insurer may have been wrong.

Penalties for bad faith are not authorized under O.C.G.A. § 33-4-6 if the insurance company has a sufficiently reasonable ground to contest the claim.[76] In *Guideone Life Ins. v. Ward*, a widow sued to collect benefits under her husband's life insurance policy. The husband had failed to pay his premium on its due date and died outside the grace period. Other evidence revealed, however, that the husband had overpaid his premium during the life of the policy. Thus, there was a fact issue as to whether the overpayments kept the policy in force beyond the grace period to include the time of death. Although the Court of Appeals remanded for

---

[74] *Lawyers Title Ins. Corp. v. Griffin*, 302 Ga. App. 726, 691 S.E.2d 633, (2010).
[75] *Lloyd's Syndicate No. 5820 v. AGCO Corp.*, ___ Ga. App. ___, 734 S.E.2d 899, 904 (2012) (denying summary judgment to insurer on bad because the court could not conclude that "the refusal to pay was reasonable as a matter of law").
[76] *Guideone Life Ins. Co. v. Ward*, 275 Ga. App. 1, 619 S.E.2d 723 (2005).

determination of the coverage issue, the court ruled that the husband's failure to pay the premium constituted a reasonable ground to contest coverage, precluding bad faith as a matter of law.

> (e)   Bad faith found if disputed issue of fact concerns a collateral issue and the insurer failed to investigate.

When a disputed question of fact regards a collateral issue, however, the insurer does not have a reasonable ground for contesting liability for damages from a covered claim. In *Georgia Farm Bureau Mut. Ins. Co. v. Murphy*,[77] the insured was driving while intoxicated, lost control of her car and hit a tree. Although a front tire was flat, she drove another 11 miles. Her right rear assembly fell off, but she continued driving another 20 miles until her car caught fire. The insured sought coverage for a total loss to her vehicle. The insurer denied, arguing that the damages stemmed from the fire rather than the impact with the tree. The insured's expert examined the car and testified that the frame was so warped by the impact with the tree that the car was totaled before it ever caught fire. The jury found in favor of the insured on coverage and awarded bad-faith damages.

The Court of Appeals affirmed, reasoning that the insurer had failed to investigate whether the car was totaled by the impact with the tree. "[A] failure upon the part of [an insurer] to investigate [an] alleged loss or damage, and a denial upon the part of the company of any liability whatsoever upon the ground that such loss or damage was not recoverable under the policy, but arose from some cause not covered by the policy, may be considered as evidence of bad faith on the part of the insurance company in refusing to pay for such loss or damage."[78] The court noted that the insurer "knew at the time the claim was investigated that the car

---

[77] 201 Ga. App. 676, 411 S.E.2d 791 (1991).
[78] *Id.* at 678, 793.

was damaged by its collision with the tree before it was damaged by the fire, and that there was no question that [the insurer] was liable under the policy for the damage stemming from that original collision." Therefore, there was no reasonable basis for the insurer's failure to investigate the extent of damage caused by the covered collision. Questions of fact regarding a collateral issue – the post-collision fire – were not a "reasonable ground" for the insurer to contest its liability for damages stemming from a covered claim.

(f)   No bad faith where there is a doubtful question of law.

In *Federal Ins. Co. v. National Distributing Co., Inc.*,[79] an alcohol distributor based in Georgia employed a Florida resident as a salesperson. The employee caused an auto accident in Florida while traveling on company business. The claimant sought punitive damages. The insurance policy provided coverage for punitive damages. Coverage for punitive damages is allowed in Georgia, but Florida courts have ruled that insurance coverage for punitive damages is contrary to public policy. The insured settled the case, and the insurer refused to indemnify the insured for the settlement amount that reflected punitive damages, arguing that Florida law applied to the issue of insurance coverage. The appellate court concluded that Georgia law applied to insurance coverage, meaning there was coverage for punitive damages. Nonetheless, the insurer was not liable for bad-faith damages as a matter of law, because the choice-of-law issue was reasonably disputed.

(g)   No bad faith for partial payment when amount of claim reasonably questioned.

In *Shaffer v. State Farm Mut. Auto. Ins. Co.*,[80] the insured was injured in an automobile accident. The insured's auto-

---

[79]   203 Ga. App. 763, 417 S.E.2d 671 (1992).
[80]   246 Ga. App. 244, 540 S.E.2d 227 (2000).

mobile policy provided for payment of reasonable medical expenses incurred as a result of automobile accidents. After the accident, the insured was transported by ambulance and treated. The insurer paid the ambulance and hospital costs. The next day, the insured saw an internist who referred her for physical therapy. The insurer paid the internist's bill but retained the services of an independent physician to determine if the physical therapy bill was excessive. The physician concluded that certain bills were excessive and that the records did not indicate the necessity of physical therapy. The physician recommended partial payment of $1,185.81, which the insurer tendered. The insured filed suit for the balance, alleging bad faith. The trial court granted partial summary judgment to the insurer on the bad-faith claim, finding the refusal to pay reasonable as a matter of law because of the advice of the independent physician.

The Court of Appeals affirmed, citing *Jones v. State Farm Mut. Auto. Ins. Co.*, which held as follows:

> The advice of an independent medical examiner that the treatment furnished a claimant is not in fact necessary treatment for injuries arising from the accident covered by the insurance policy, unless patently wrong based on facts timely brought to the insurer's attention, provides a reasonable basis for an insurer's denial of a claim for payment of such treatment.[81]

(h)   No bad faith where insured recovers substantially less than demanded, but insurance company acknowledges coverage.

Where the verdict in a suit on an insurance policy is for substantially less than the amount claimed in the proof of loss and less than the amount demanded in the petition, no recovery for bad-faith damages and attorney's fees is autho-

---

[81]   228 Ga. App. 347, 350-351, 491 S.E.2d 830 (1997).

rized.[82] In *Georgia Farm Bur. Mut. Ins. Co. v. Boney*, the insured purchased a new car for $2,400 and rolled it five days
later. The insured submitted a proof of loss for $2,350, the
cost of the car less the $50 deductible. The insurance com-
pany acknowledged coverage but refused to pay the amount
sought. Rather, the insurance company offered to (1) have
the car repaired by the insured's choice of dealer or (2) pay
$800. The insured rejected the offer, sent a 60-day demand
for $1,400 and filed suit. The jury awarded $1,000 for the
loss as well as a bad-faith penalty. The Court of Appeals reversed the bad-faith award, ruling that there can be no bad
faith as a matter of law where the proof of loss seeks $2,350,
the insured seeks $1,400 in its petition, and the jury awards
$1,000. The court found it significant that the insurance
company had gathered several estimates "from reputable
people engaged in the repairing of automobiles." In addition, the insured refused to produce the damaged car or
meaningfully cooperate with the appraisal process called for
in the policy.

(i)   Bad faith even though insured recovers less
       than demanded, but insurance company had
       denied all coverage.

In *Hendley v. Am. Nat'l Fire Ins. Co.*,[83] the insured's home
was damaged by a storm. The insurer denied all coverage,
asserting that the insured had failed to give timely notice or
make repairs to protect her property from additional damage immediately after the storm. The insured sought approximately $117,000 in damages but recovered much less.
The issue on appeal was whether the issue of bad faith
should have gone to the jury "where the jury awarded only
59% of the damages which [the insured] requested."[84] The
Eleventh Circuit distinguished between, on the one hand,
cases where the insured recovered substantially less than

---

[82] *Georgia Farm Bur. Mut. Ins. Co. v. Boney*, 113 Ga. App. 459, 148 S.E.
2d 457 (1966).
[83] 842 F. 2d 267, 268 (11th Cir. 1988).
[84] *Id.* at 268.

the amount demanded but the insurer had acknowledged coverage with, on the other hand, cases where the insured recovered less than the amount demanded but the insurer had denied coverage. In the former, the insurance company can escape bad faith as a matter of law if it shows good cause for the dispute. In the latter, the issue of bad faith is for the jury.[85]

In addition, the Eleventh Circuit noted that "[t]he fact that the parties have a dispute as to liability will not preclude liability for bad faith penalties."[86] Although acknowledging that the insurance company's defenses "provided a genuine dispute," the Eleventh Circuit refused to find that there could be no bad faith as a matter of law. "Only a very finely-drawn distinction separates the insufficient defense from the one which as a matter of law raises a reasonable question of law or a reasonable issue of fact."[87]

Other cases have found that if the insurer has completely denied any liability, the insured's failure to recover the full amount sued for will not preclude an insured from recovering a penalty and attorneys' fees for bad faith.[88]

> (j)   Bad faith is for the jury where there is a dispute as to whether the insurer's offer of payment was unreasonably low.

Where an insured has suffered a loss, efforts by the insurance company to settle the claim that are not bona fide can be a constructive refusal to pay.[89] In *Firemen's Ins. Co. of*

---

[85] *Id.* at 270 (collecting cases and explaining distinction).
[86] *Id.* at 269, quoting *Colonial Life & Accident Ins. Co. v. McLain*, 243 Ga. 263 (1979).
[87] *Id.* at 270.
[88] *Hanover Ins. Co. v. Hallford*, 127 Ga. App. 322, 324, 193 S.E.2d 235 (1972), citing *Central Mfrs. Mut. Ins. Co. v. Graham*, 24 Ga. App. 199, 99 S.E. 434 (1919); *New York Life Ins. Co. v. Williamson*, 53 Ga. App. 28, 38, 184 S.E. 755 (1936); and *Canal Ins. Co. v. Winge Bros.*, 97 Ga. App. 782, 786, 104 S.E.2d 525 (1958).
[89] 105 Ga. App. 763, 766-67, 125 S.E. 2d 545, 548 (1962).

Newark, N.J. v. Allmond, the insurance company acknowledged coverage, made an offer of settlement of $2,250, and a jury determined the amount of the loss to have been $4,000. In such a case, "it was a question for the jury to say whether the offer had been so small as to amount to an absolute refusal to pay, and if so, whether there was bad faith in such refusal."[90] Accordingly, the Court of Appeals affirmed the jury's award of bad-faith damages.

> (k)   Seeking a judicial declaration on a disputed coverage issue does not defeat bad faith as a matter of law.

"[T]he mere filing of a declaratory judgment action does not in and of itself absolve an insurer from being subject to a bad faith penalty under O.C.G.A. § 33-4-6." [91] In *Great Southwest Exp. Co. Inc. v. Great Am. Ins. Co. of New York*, the insured filed a claim that the insurer disputed. The insurance company filed a declaratory judgment action against its insured, seeking direction from a court as to whether coverage existed. The insured counterclaimed for coverage and bad-faith damages. The trial court denied the insurance company's motion for summary judgment on bad faith, and the Court of Appeals affirmed, holding that the issue of bad faith was for the jury.

Likewise, there are circumstances when the insurance company's failure to seek a declaratory judgment can be evidence of bad faith.[92]

---

[90] *Id.* at 767, 549.

[91] *Great Southwest Exp. Co. Inc. v. Great Am. Ins. Co. of New York*, 292 Ga. App. 757, 761, 665 S.E. 2d 878, 881 (2008), cert. denied, Nov. 3, 2008.

[92] *First Financial Ins. Co. v. Am. Sandblasting Co.*, 223 Ga. App. 232, 233, 477 S.E. 2d 390, 392 (1996) (allowing bad faith to go to the jury because, in part, the insurance company "failed to follow the recommended procedure for contesting coverage [seeking a declaratory judgment] in cases like this").

(1)   An insurer's waiver of a coverage defense does not preclude bad faith.

An insurance company that retains a prepaid premium for four and one-half years after learning of fraudulent answers in the insurance application may waive the defense that the policy was void ab initio, but the insurer may still maintain the fraud defense to the bad faith claim.[93]   In *Florida Int'l Indem. Co. v. Osgood*, the insured's house burned. The insurer discovered that the insured had committed fraud in the application by failing to inform the insurer of previous losses by fire. Rather than rescinding the policy, the insurer issued a notice of nonrenewal that specifically stated that the policy remained in effect. The court determined that the notice waived the right to rely on the defense of fraud with regard to coverage. However, because "[t]he waiver did not eliminate the fact that [the insured] had defrauded [the insurer]," a directed verdict for the insurer on bad faith was appropriate.[94]

§ 2.5   STATUTE OF LIMITATIONS

Actions upon written contracts must be brought within six years.[95]   The six-year period of limitations applies to insurance policies.[96]   On its face, O.C.G.A. § 33-4-6 does not include its own statute of limitations. The six-year statute of limitations for simple written contracts applies to bad-faith actions, because the action is "based upon rights arising from [the] contract of insurance."[97]   Care should be taken,

---

[93]   *Florida Int'l Indem. Co. v. Osgood*, 233 Ga. App. 111, 115, 503 S.E.2d 371, 374 (1998).

[94]   *Florida Int'l Indem. Co. v. Osgood*, 233 Ga. App. 111, 116, 503 S.E.2d 371, 375 (1998).

[95]   O.C.G.A. § 9-3-24.

[96]   *Childs v. Armour Food Co.*, 175 Ga. App. 455, 455, 333 S.E.2d 377 (1985).

[97]   *See Sentry Ins. Co. v. Echols*, 174 Ga. App. 541, 543, 330 S.E.2d 725 (1985).

however, because some insurance policies contain contractual terms that effectively limit the statute of limitations.[98]

§ 2.6　AMOUNT OF THE BAD-FAITH PENALTY

If the insured proves that the insurer acted in bad faith, the insured is entitled to recover "in addition to the loss, not more than 50 percent of the liability of the insurer for the loss or $5,000.00, whichever is greater."[99]　The Court of Appeals has held that if bad faith is found to exist, the amount of bad-faith damages can be determined by the trial court as a matter of law based solely on the amount of the insured loss.[100]　The insurance company had argued on appeal that the amount of bad-faith damages should be left to the jury, which could award as bad-faith damages "up to" 50 percent of the loss or $5,000, whichever is greater.　The Court of Appeals disagreed, holding that "[t]he clear language of the statute provided for a payment of either 50 percent of the amount of the loss ... or $5,000, whichever was greater."[101] The court further wrote that the insurance company's "argument to the contrary is based on an inaccurate parsing of the statute."[102]　Arguably, however, the reasoning in *Atlantic Title Ins. Co. v. Aegis Funding Corp.* fails to take into account the phrase "not more than" that appears in the statute and adds the word "either," which does not appear in the statute.　In addition, physical precedent indicates that the Court of Appeals has approved bad-faith verdicts in amounts lower than the applicable percentage set forth in the statute.[103]

---

[98]　*See* § 5.8, *infra.*, discussing "No Action Clauses."

[99]　O.C.G.A. § 33-4-6(a).

[100]　*Atlantic Title Ins. Co. v. Aegis Funding Corp.*, 287 Ga. App. 392, 396, 651 S.E. 2d 507, 510 (2007) (approving finding of bad faith as a matter of law based on insurance company's insufficient actions in investigating a loss covered under the clear terms of a title insurance policy), *cert. denied*, Jan. 28, 2008.

[101]　*Id.* at 396, 510 (emphasis added).

[102]　*Id.*

[103]　*E.g., Firemen's Ins. Co. of Newark, N.J. v. Allmond*, 105 Ga. App. 763, 125 S.E. 2d 545 (1962) (affirming bad-faith award of 15 percent of damages at time Georgia's bad-faith statute allowed up to 25 percent).

If a single "loss" is comprised of many small amounts total-
ing less than $10,000 (for example, multiple medical bills
resulting from a single accident), only a single $5,000 penal-
ty is appropriate rather than a separate $5,000 penalty for
each medical bill the insurance company failed to pay.[104]

§ 2.7 ATTORNEY FEES

O.C.G.A. § 33-4-6 expressly states that "[t]he amount of any
reasonable attorney's fees shall be determined by the trial
jury and shall be included in any judgment which is rendered in the action." Thus, even in cases where the court
finds that the insurance company acted in bad faith as a
matter of law and awards the bad-faith penalty, the issue of
attorney's fees goes to the jury.[105] Although the statute gives
the trial court "discretion, if [the trial court] finds the jury
verdict fixing attorney's fees to be greatly excessive or inadequate, to review and amend the portion of the verdict fixing attorney's fees," the failure to submit the issue of fees to
the jury in the first instance is reversible error.[106]

The statute bases the amount of the attorney fee award on
"the reasonable value of the services based on the time spent
and legal and factual issues involved in accordance with
prevailing fees in the locality where the action is pending."[107]
An award of fees may be in excess of the amount of the insured loss, so long as it is reasonable under the circumstances.[108] *Reserve Life Ins. Co. v. Ayers* involved hospital insurance for loss caused by illness. The plaintiff got sick and
incurred hospital bills that the insurance company did not
pay. The plaintiff sued the insurance company and was
awarded $565.10 as unpaid benefits. The insured's attorney

---

[104] *Byrd v. Regal Ins. Co.*, 275 Ga. App. 779, 621 S.E. 2d 758 (2005).
[105] *Atlantic Title Ins. Co. v. Aegis Funding Corp.*, 287 Ga. App. 392, 396,
651 S.E. 2d 507, 510 (2007), *cert. denied*, Jan. 28, 2008.
[106] *Transportation Ins. Co. v. Piedmont Construction Group, LLC*, 301 Ga.
App. 17, 686 S.E. 2d 824 (2009), *cert. denied*, March 29, 2010.
[107] O.C.G.A. § 33-4-6(a).
[108] *Reserve Life Ins. Co. v. Ayers*, 217 Ga. 206, 121 S.E.2d 649 (1961).

testified that he had expended "great effort" in litigating the claim, preparing the complaint and several amendments and trying the case twice. After the first trial the case had gone up to the court of appeals and come back for a second trial. The attorney also had to make several trips that entailed considerable expense. He estimated the value of his services at $9,293.62. The jury found bad faith and awarded $8,000.00 in attorney's fees. The Supreme Court of Georgia rejected the notion that the award was "clearly excessive in view of the amount of the principal sued for."[109]

The statute also requires that any award of attorney fees "shall be fixed on the basis of competent expert evidence."[110] The authors are aware of no reported decision from the Court of Appeals stating that the attorney prosecuting the case may not be his or her own expert and testify about their fees "standing in their place." In some courts, practitioners are being allowed to present such evidence "standing in their place" while others are designating third-party experts. The authors urge litigants to consider how fees are to be proved early in the litigation. Presentation by an objective expert that explains the reasonable costs of the legal services rendered may be more persuasive to a jury.

If there is a finding of bad faith in the trial court, attorneys' fees incurred defending the finding on appeal are also awardable under O.C.G.A. § 33-4-6.[111] In such a case, the appellate court should direct the trial court to conduct further proceedings for the purpose of assessing post-trial fees.[112]

§ 2.8   EXCLUSIVE REMEDY

As to statutory bad faith, the penalties contained in O.C.G.A. § 33-4-6 are the exclusive remedies for an insurer's

---

[109] *Id.* at 211, 653.
[110] O.C.G.A. § 33-4-6(a).
[111] *Am. Assoc. of Cab Cos. Inc. v. Olukoya*, 233 Ga. App. 731, 505 S.E. 2d 761 (1998), *cert. denied*, Dec. 4, 1998.
[112] *Id.*

bad faith refusal to pay insurance proceeds.[113]   In *Great Southwest Exp. Co. Inc. v. Great Am. Ins. Co. of New York,* the insured was a common carrier whose biggest customer was Goodyear Tire and Rubber Company.   Several trailers loaded with tires were stolen from the insured's premises. The common carrier's property insurer denied coverage, arguing that an "unattended vehicle exclusion" barred coverage.   The insured disputed whether the exclusion was part of the policy.   During the coverage dispute, Goodyear stopped doing business with the common carrier, forcing the common carrier out of business.   In the ensuing coverage litigation, the insured sought lost profits and punitive damages.   The Court of Appeals approved the trial court's grant of summary judgment against the common carrier on that issue, reasoning that the insured's recovery was limited to its damages under the bad-faith statute: "[A]bsent some special relationship beyond the relation of insurer and insured, O.C.G.A. § 33-4-6 provides the exclusive remedy."[114]

Similarly, allegations that a fire insurer delayed payment in bad faith does not entitle an insured to additional living expenses or other consequential damages not provided for in the policy or otherwise recoverable under O.C.G.A. § 33-4-6.[115]   The bad-faith statute is the exclusive remedy for an insurance company's bad faith failure to pay, precluding recovery for attorneys' fees under O.C.G.A. § 13-6-11 and O.C.G.A. § 9-15-14.[116]

---

[113]   *Great Southwest Exp. Co. Inc. v. Great Am. Ins. Co. of New York,* 292 Ga. App. 757, 760, 665 S.E. 2d 878, 881 (2008), *cert. denied,* Nov. 3, 2008.

[114]   *Id.* at n. 3.

[115]   *Anderson v. Georgia Farm Bureau Mut. Ins. Co.,* 255 Ga. App. 734, 566 S.E. 2d 342 (2002), *cert. denied,* Sept. 30. 2002.

[116]   *Adams v. Unum Life Ins. Co. of America,* 508 F. Supp. 1302, 1319 (N.D. Ga. 2007), citing *United Services Auto Ass'n v. Carroll,* 226 Ga. App. 144, 148, 486 S.E.2d 613 (1997) and *Howell v. Southern Heritage Ins. Co.,* 214 Ga. App. 536, 448 S.E.2d 275 (1994) ("Georgia case law … clearly establishes that O.C.G.A. § 33-4-6 is the exclusive remedy for an insurer's bad faith refusal to pay insurance proceeds, and that claims for attorney's fees and litigation expenses under other Georgia statutes are not authorized.")

§ 2.9   ASSIGNABILITY

Several courts have held that the right to recover penalties and attorneys' fees under O.C.G.A. § 33-4-6 belongs to the insured and is not assignable.[117] Other courts have stated, without holding, that the opposite is true.[118] A third-party claimant cannot step into the place of the insured and recover under the bad-faith statute.[119] "Although it is also possible to construe O.C.G.A. § 33-4-6 as referring exclusively to [] the named holder of the insurance policy, a construction of the statute which recognizes the assignee of benefits as the holder of the policy is preferable under the present facts [assignment of insurance benefits by patient to hospital] because it conforms the operation of the statute to the common law applicable to assignments."[120]

§ 2.10   BAD FAITH AND CLAIMS BY A THIRD PARTY FOR PROPERTY DAMAGE TO AUTOMOBILE

A statute modeled after O.C.G.A. § 33-4-6 provides a remedy for third parties with claims for property damage under a tortfeasor's automobile liability policy.[121] O.C.G.A. § 33-4-7(a) provides:

---

[117] *Southern General Ins. Co. v. Ross*, 227 Ga. App. 191, 196, 489 S.E.2d 53 (1997) and *Canal Indem. Co. v. Greene*, 265 Ga. App. 67, 72, 593 S.E.2d 41, 46 (2003) (distinguishing between the nonassignability of statutory bad-faith claims and the assignability of bad-faith claims under the common law).

[118] *Blue Cross & Blue Shield of Georgia, Inc. v. Bennett*, 223 Ga. App. 291, 292, 477 S.E.2d 442, 444 (1996) ("After Bennett assigned the right to the benefits at issue to St. Joseph's Hospital, the hospital, in effect, became the holder of the policy for all purposes related to enforcing the right to the assigned benefits under the policy, including the right to demand payment of the assigned benefits under OCGA § 33-4-6.").

[119] *Owens v. Allstate Ins. Co.*, 216 Ga. App. 650, 651, 455 S.E.2d 368 (1995); *Southern General Ins. Co. v. Ross*, 227 Ga. App. 191, 196, 489 S.E.2d 53 (1997).

[120] *Blue Cross & Blue Shield of Georgia, Inc. v. Bennett*, 223 Ga. App. 291, 292, 477 S.E.2d 442, 444 (1996).

[121] *King v. Atlanta Cas. Ins. Co.*, 279 Ga. App. 554, 556, 631 S.E.2d 786 (2006) ("Given the similarity between the two statutes, we find the case law applying O.C.G.A. § 33-4-6 to be persuasive here.") citing *Fortson v. Cotton States Mut. Ins. Co.*, 168 Ga. App. 155, 157, 308 S.E.2d 382 (1983).

In the event of a loss because of injury to or destruction of property covered by a motor vehicle liability insurance policy, the insurer issuing such policy has an affirmative duty to adjust that loss fairly and promptly, to make a reasonable effort to investigate and evaluate the claim, and, where liability is reasonably clear, to make a good faith effort to settle with the claimant potentially entitled to recover against the insured under such policy. Any insurer who breaches this duty may be liable to pay the claimant, in addition to the loss, not more than 50 percent of the liability of the insured for the loss or $5,000.00, whichever is greater, and all reasonable attorney's fees for the prosecution of the action.

The statute has its own 60-day demand requirement, requiring the third party to demand an "amount certain" via certified mail or statutory overnight delivery.[122] If the demand is not paid within 60 days, the claimant may proceed against the insurer, who will be an unnamed party.[123] If the claimant recovers more than or equal to the amount of the demand, the trial shall be recommenced to determine the insurer's bad faith.[124]

A third party cannot bring an action against an insurer under this statute for failure to make a good-faith effort to settle a personal injury claim as opposed to a property loss.[125]

§ 2.11 BAD FAITH AND UM CLAIMS

Another statute modeled after O.C.G.A. § 33-4-6 provides a remedy for insureds who are improperly denied uninsured or underinsured motorist benefits. "UM" coverage is an optional coverage that an insured may purchase to cover the insured who is injured by the negligence of another person

---

[122] O.C.G.A. § 33-4-7(c).
[123] O.C.G.A. § 33-4-7(d).
[124] O.C.G.A. § 33-4-7(d).
[125] *Mills v. Allstate Ins. Co.*, 288 Ga. App. 257, 653 S.E.2d 850 (2007).

who has no liability coverage or insufficient liability coverage to compensate the insured for his or her injuries. O.C.G.A. § 33-7-11(j) provides:

> If the insurer shall refuse to pay any insured any loss covered by this Code section within 60 days after a demand has been made by the insured and a finding has been made that such refusal was made in bad faith, the insurer shall be liable to the insured in addition to any recovery under this Code section for not more than 25 percent of the recovery and all reasonable attorney's fees for the prosecution of the case under this Code section. The question of bad faith, the amount of the penalty, if any, and the reasonable attorney's fees, if any, shall be determined in a separate action filed by the insured against the insurer after a judgment has been rendered against the uninsured motorist in the original tort action. The attorney's fees shall be fixed on the basis of competent expert evidence as to the reasonable value of the services, based on the time spent and legal and factual issues involved, in accordance with prevailing fees in the locality where the action is pending. The trial court shall have the discretion, if it finds such jury verdict fixing attorney's fees to be greatly excessive or inadequate, to review and amend such portion of the verdict fixing attorney's fees without the necessity of disapproving the entire verdict. The limitations contained in this subsection in reference to the amount of attorney's fees are not controlling as to the fees which may be agreed upon by the plaintiff and his attorney for the services of the attorney in the action against the insurer.

Unlike the other bad-faith statutes, the one applicable to UM carriers contemplates two lawsuits. The first against the uninsured or underinsured tortfeasor, fixing liability, and a second against the insured's UM carrier. It is clear that an insured plaintiff must obtain a judgment against the uninsured motorist [pursuant to other subsections of O.C.G.A. § 33-7-11] before filing suit against the UM carrier.[126] It does not follow, however, that the insured must make its 60-day demand to the UM carrier prior to that lawsuit.[127] The Supreme Court of Georgia has ruled that the purpose of the statute is to encourage insurers to make a good-faith examination of claims and to promptly pay all valid claims. The purpose would not be fulfilled if the UM carrier did not have to evaluate the claim until liability is fixed in the lawsuit against the uninsured tortfeasor. Rather, the UM carrier must evaluate the claim upon demand so as to create a possibility that no action against the uninsured tortfeasor is necessary and that the insured victim be compensated.[128]

The penalty of "25 percent of the recovery" refers to the amount of UM coverage, not the recovery against the uninsured tortfeasor.[129]

An insured is not entitled to recover damages from its UM carrier for the tortfeasor's bad faith and stubborn litigiousness in the insured's action against the tortfeasor.[130] The statute provides a cause of action for the policyholder who has UM coverage, not for the underinsured motorist subject to a lawsuit that the UM carrier had an opportunity to settle.[131]

[126] *Lewis v. Cherokee Ins. Co.*, 258 Ga. 839, 375 S.E. 2d 850 (1989).
[127] *Id.*
[128] *Id.*
[129] *Jones v. Cotton States Mut. Ins. Co.*, 185 Ga. App. 66, 70, 363 S.E. 2d 303, 307 (1987), *cert. denied*, Jan. 14, 1988.
[130] *Smith v. Stoddard*, 294 Ga. App. 679, 669 S.E. 2d 712 (2008).
[131] *See Nationwide Mut. Ins. Co. v. Turner*, 135 Ga. App. 551, 218 S.E. 2d 276 (1975).

CHAPTER 3

COMMON-LAW BAD FAITH

§ 3.1 INTRODUCTION

In addition to the cause of action for bad-faith failure to pay that is grounded in *statute*,[1] Georgia recognizes a cause of action for insurance bad faith that is grounded in the *common law*. As explained below, common-law bad faith is associated with a liability insurer's fiduciary duty to protect its insured from the risks associated with litigation against the insured. In most cases, these risks include legal liability to the insured for damages the insured has allegedly caused to a third-party claimant. Succinctly stated, "[a]n insurance company may be liable for damages to its insured for failing to settle the claim of an injured person where the insurer is guilty of negligence, fraud, or bad faith in failing to compromise the claim."[2] The most common example of an insurance company's liability for bad faith arises when the insurance company fails to take advantage of a reasonable opportunity to settle claims against its insured within policy limits.[3]

§ 3.2 ORIGINS AND THE *SMOOT* TRILOGY

The Georgia Court of Appeals summarized the common-law duty of good faith in *dicta* more than 60 years ago, noting that a liability insurer "may be held liable for damages to its insured for failing to adjust or compromise a claim covered by its policy of insurance, where the insurer is guilty of negligence or of fraud or bad faith in failing to adjust or compromise the claim to the injury of the insured."[4] While this

---

[1] O.C.G.A. § 33-4-6. *See* § 2, *supra*.

[2] *Southern General Ins. Co, v. Holt*, 262 Ga. 267, 268, 416 S.E.2d 274, 276 (1992).

[3] *Cotton States Mut. Ins. Co. v. Brightman*, 276 Ga. 683, 685, 580 S.E.2d 519 (2003).

[4] *Francis v. Newton*, 75 Ga. App. 341, 344, 43 S.E.2d 282 (1947).

statement of the law endures today, it was the former Fifth Circuit Court of Appeals, applying Georgia law, that gave firm shape to the concept. From 1962 to 1967, the Fifth Circuit issued three decisions in the matter of *Smoot v. State Farm Mutual Automobile Insurance Company.*[5] These cases set forth the "the good faith doctrine," which describes the duties of the liability insurer to investigate, adjust, and, in the proper case, settle claims against the insured. A detailed examination of the *Smoot* trilogy is a highly instructive primer to the law of common-law bad faith.

The *Smoot* cases arose from a 1955 automobile accident. Sergeant Smoot was insured by State Farm on an automobile liability policy with limits of $10,000 per person and $20,000 per accident. In November 1955, Smoot was driving, not paying attention and rear-ended Katie Mae Donaldson. The accident involved five cars and was severe enough to knock one of Donaldson's passengers to the floor of the car. Smoot notified State Farm of the accident and State Farm took a statement from him. Three months after the accident he was assigned to military duty in Guam.

In March 1956, Donaldson's attorney provided State Farm with a medical report showing that Donaldson had received a severe whiplash injury that was generally improving. Her attorney made an oral offer to settle for $2,500. Her attorney later made a written settlement demand for $4,000. State Farm rejected both offers. In July 1956, Donaldson's attorney communicated to State Farm that Donaldson's symptoms were reoccurring. State Farm had Donaldson examined by a doctor, and the examination revealed continuing symptoms. Donaldson's attorney demanded $5,000 to settle but State Farm rejected it. None of these settlement offers and refusals was communicated to Smoot.

---

[5] *Smoot v. State Farm Mut. Auto. Ins. Co.,* 299 F.2d 525 (5th Cir. 1962) ("Smoot I"); 337 F.2d 223 (5th Cir. 1964) ("Smoot II"); 381 F.2d 331 (5th Cir. 1967) ("Smoot III").

Finally, Mrs. Donaldson and her husband filed separate suits against Smoot, claiming $33,980 and $2,922.83 in damages, respectively. Mrs. Donaldson demanded $5,000 to settle the case and her husband demanded his full amount of damages. State Farm sent Smoot a letter indicating that it had hired attorneys to represent him in the suits. The letter contained the following language:

> Because of the fact that the amount claimed against you in these suits is in excess of the protection afforded by this policy, there may be a personal liability upon your part. In view of the possible personal liability, it will be agreeable with this company and its representatives for you, if you so elect, to procure attorneys of your own choosing, at your own expense, to represent you personally and appear in this matter, in addition to the attorneys we have selected and will compensate.

State Farm also secured a stay of the suits pending Smoot's return from Guam. Smoot returned to Georgia in early 1958. In March 1958, the court ruled against Smoot and State Farm on the issue of whether service upon Smoot had been valid. State Farm's attorneys failed to have a transcript or a certificate made and therefore were unable to appeal the ruling.

Shortly before the trial, State Farm offered to settle both of the Donaldsons' cases for $5,000, but the Donaldsons refused. Mrs. Donaldson's doctors re-examined her, but State Farm failed to obtain the results of the examinations. At trial, two doctors testifying for the defense confirmed the nature and extent of Mrs. Donaldson's injuries. State Farm knew the doctors would testify unfavorably but did nothing to counteract it. During jury deliberations, one of the attorneys hired by State Farm discussed the possibility of an excess verdict with the Donaldsons' attorney. He even mentioned the letter that State Farm wrote to Smoot claiming that the letter "took care" of the issue. After judgment was entered on the jury verdict of $26,902.83 (an amount in excess of policy limits), State Farm's attorneys filed a motion for new trial but failed to file the supporting brief of evidence. The motion automatically failed and the case concluded.

Smoot then filed suit against State Farm for damages, seeking the amount that the judgments against him exceeded policy limits. State Farm removed to Federal court and filed a motion to dismiss for failure to state a claim, which was granted by the district court. The Fifth Circuit reversed ("Smoot I"). State Farm then added the Donaldsons as indispensable parties and pled accord and satisfaction. The jury found in favor of State Farm and Smoot appealed. The Fifth Circuit again reversed and remanded and directed a trial solely between Smoot and State Farm ("Smoot II").

After the second remand, the jury returned a special verdict finding (1) State Farm was negligent in the manner in which it carried out its obligation to the insured under the auto policy; (2) the negligence resulted in damage to Smoot; (3) State Farm was guilty of bad faith in the manner in which it carried out its obligations as insurer; (4) State Farm's bad faith damaged Smoot; (5) Smoot was entitled to special damages of $23,858.40; (6) Smoot was entitled to general damages of $10,000; (7) Smoot was entitled to punitive damages of $10,000; and (8) Smoot was entitled to recover attorneys' fees of $21,929.20. A general verdict of $65,787.60 was entered. State Farm appealed again, and the Fifth Circuit affirmed ("*Smoot III*").

The result in *Smoot* makes sense when viewed in context of the development of liability insurance. Under the earliest liability policies, the insurer agreed only to indemnify the insured if the insured was subject to a judgment and the insured actually paid the judgment. Later, some insurers expanded coverage, agreeing to pay the judgment on behalf of the insured as soon as it was rendered, removing the requirement that the insured pay the judgment first. To make their product more attractive (and to protect themselves from the risk of high judgments), some insurers also agreed to provide a defense to the insured. Thus, under older policies, an insurer might not become involved in a lawsuit against the insured until and unless a judgment was actually entered against the insured. In the newer policies, the insurer charged a premium for promising to get involved and protect the insured as soon as the insured faced potential legal liability.

Today, the typical liability insurance contract expressly states that the insurer *will* indemnify and *may* settle.[6] By use of the word "may," and similar constructions, the insurer reserves for itself discretion as to whether the case is worth settling. Thus, the insurer totally controls the decision to settle and, therefore, whether and under what terms to protect the insured against a financially injurious judgment. The Fifth Circuit in *Smoot I* expressly recognized that the insurer had taken a premium not just to pay a sum certain if the insured was adjudged liable for damages. The insurer was accepting advance payment to use its skill, experience and resources in protecting the insured (and itself) from the risk of potential legal liability. This distinction is not borne from any public policy or championship of individuals over big companies, but from the words the insurer used in drafting its policy. The liability insurer's decision to keep exclusive control over the decision to settle claims imports to the insurer the corresponding duty to make such decisions non-negligently and in good faith.

Within this context, the court ruled that "[t]he allegations were quite sufficient to charge want of good faith in rejecting settlement offers within the policy limits and generally in the

---

[6] A typical liability policy includes the following: "We *will* pay those sums that the insured becomes legally obligated to pay . . . We *will* have the right and duty to defend the insured . . . We *may, at our discretion*, investigate any "occurrence" and settle any claim." CG 00 01 10 01, © ISO Properties, Inc., 2000 (emphasis added).

handling of the defense."[7] The complaint could not be dismissed at its early stages, according to the panel, because of the intensely factual nature of an analysis under the "good faith doctrine." Foreshadowing the development of Georgia law in this area, the former Fifth Circuit explained that "[b]y its very nature that question [the insurer's good faith] encompasses the more specific ones concerning the reasonable valuation of the case, whether, at each stage, proposed settlements were rejected consciously in terms of deliberative judgment evaluation or because of other or no reasons."[8] For this reason, discovery in bad-faith lawsuits often focuses on whether the insurer promptly and thoroughly investigated the liability case against the insured and the damages alleged to have been caused by the insured so as to be able to reasonably evaluate such proposed settlements.

The insurance company's "deliberative judgment" and "evaluation" could be at issue, because "the whole thing was being directed by adjusters or other functionaries" who must have sufficient judgment and ability to direct or choose a prudent course of action.[9] Thus, while performing duties it undertook under the insurance contract, the insurer must "determine in intelligent good faith just what the case was worth in terms of the probabilities of success or failure."[10] If the insurer failed in its promise to use its litigation expertise, investigative resources and prudent discretion to protect its insured, and if the insured was damaged thereby, the insured had the basis of an action in tort.[11] The Fifth Circuit in *Smoot I* understood that the contractual duty the insurance company had undertaken in agreeing to defend, while retaining for itself the discretionary power to settle, created duties in tort as well.

---

[7]   *Smoot I*, 299 F.2d at 531.
[8]   *Id.* 299 F.2d at 531.
[9]   *Id.* 299 F.2d at 533-34.
[10]   *Id.* 299 F.2d at 533-34.
[11]   *Id.* 299 F.2d at 528.

§ 3.3   THE EQUAL CONSIDERATION RULE

The "Equal Consideration Rule" provides the standard by which an insurance company's decision to not settle a claim against its insured is measured. The standard was pronounced five years after *Smoot I*, when the Georgia Court of Appeals in *United States Fidelity & Guar. Co. v. Evans* expressly recognized that a cause of action against a liability insurer for failing in its duties to properly protect its insured arises "in tort and naturally involves a duty and an alleged breach of that duty."[12] Deciding that a duty exists begs the question, however, which the court itself asked: "What then is the duty?"[13] The answer to that question, which is the holding in *Evans*, is best understood in its factual context. The underlying lawsuit in *Evans* was a typical car-wreck case resulting in a verdict against the insured in excess of policy limits.[14] Following the verdict, the claimant offered to settle for policy limits, apparently preferring quick and certain payment over waiting for an appeal to run its course. The insurer refused, lost the appeal for a new trial and tendered policy limits, leaving the insured "holding the bag" for the amount in excess of policy limits. The insured filed suit against the insurer, and a jury found bad faith, entitling the insured to the difference between the judgment and policy limits. The insurer appealed, arguing that it should not be penalized for exercising its right to appeal a judgment.

The issue of law for the *Evans* court was whether there could be bad faith if the insurer's decision to appeal the underlying lawsuit was not frivolous. The insurer had argued that it could not be liable as a matter of law for failure to settle so long as its decision not to settle was supported by a

---

[12] *United States Fidelity & Guar. Co. v. Evans*, 116 Ga. App. 93, 94, 156 S.E.2d 809 (1967), *aff'd.*, 223 Ga. 789 (1967).

[13] *Id.* 116 Ga. App. at 94.

[14] The phrase "underlying lawsuit" refers to the lawsuit between the insured and the claimant and is used to distinguish between the bad-faith lawsuit between the insured and the insurance company.

non-frivolous defense pursued on behalf of the insured. The court rejected the standard, suggesting that such an analysis would turn on whether the insurer had sufficiently "consult[ed] its own self interest" in rejecting the settlement offer and deciding to assert the defense on appeal.[15] Such a standard was inadequate, the court reasoned, because it would require no analysis as to whether the insurer had consulted the *insured's* interests. Noting that the insurer must do more than merely refrain from making frivolous decisions while handling litigation against its insured, the court held as follows:

> As a professional in the defense of suits, [the insurer handling the defense] must use a degree of skill commensurate with such professional standards. As the champion of the insured, [the insurer] must consider as paramount his interests, rather than its own, and may not gamble with his funds.[16]

Stated differently, the court wrote as follows:

> [T]he insurer must accord the interest of its insured the same faithful consideration it gives its own interest. While this rule will not be as simple to apply in differing circumstances . . . we think it states the duty owed by any prudent insurer to refrain from taking an unreasonable risk on behalf of its insured, *e.g.*, where the chances of unfavorable results on appeal are out of proportion to the chances of favorable results.[17]

Applied to the facts at issue in *Evans*, the Court of Appeals held that it could not, as a matter of law, reverse the jury's determination that the insurer had failed to accord its insured's interests equal consideration to its own. Indeed, the

---

[15] *United States Fidelity & Guar. Co. v. Evans*, 116 Ga. App. 93, 95, 156 S.E.2d 809 (1967), *aff'd.*, 223 Ga. 789 (1967).

[16] *Id.* 116 Ga. App. at 95.

[17] *Id.* 116 Ga. App. at 96-97 (internal citations omitted).

court reasoned that the insurer was the only party who could possibly benefit from the appeal, as a successful appeal would only subject the insured to another trial and another opportunity to be subject to a judgment in excess of policy limits.[18] A reasonable jury could find that the insurer had failed to consider its insured's interests in refusing to settle within policy limits, cap everyone's damages, and remove the insured's risk of future liability exposure.

The Georgia Supreme Court affirmed *Evans* with little discussion. Almost 20 years later, Georgia's highest court approved *Evans* and expressly held as follows:

> An automobile liability insurance company may be liable for damages to its insured for failing to adjust or compromise the claim of a person injured by the insured and covered by its liability policy, where the insurer is guilty of negligence or of fraud or bad faith in failing to adjust or compromise the claim to the injury of the insured. Hence, where a person injured by the insured offers to settle for a sum within the policy limits, and the insurer refuses the offer of settlement, the insurer may be liable to the insured to pay the verdict rendered against the insured even though the verdict exceeds the policy limits of liability. The reason for this rule is that the insurer may not gamble with the funds of its insured by refusing to settle within the policy limits.[19]

In determining whether to settle a claim, an insurance company must give its insured's interests "equal consideration." The Georgia Supreme Court described the "equal consideration rule" as follows:

---

[18] *Id.* 116 Ga. App. at 96-97.

[19] *McCall v. Allstate Ins. Co.*, 251 Ga. 869, 870, 310 S.E.2d 513 (1984) (internal citations omitted).

> In deciding whether to settle a claim within the policy limits, the insurance company must give equal consideration to the interests of the insured. The jury generally must decide whether the insurer, in view of the existing circumstances, has accorded the insured "the same faithful consideration it gives its own interest."[20]

The "equal consideration" rule has been stated in many different ways over the years. Its significance, however, is not in the terminology used, but in the definition of the care to be exercised by the insurer. An insured may recover for the insurer's failure to settle within policy limits if the insurer (1) failed to give equal consideration to the interests of the insured;[21] (2) failed to accord its insured the same faithful consideration it accords its own interests;[22] (3) refused to settle because of an arbitrary or capricious belief that the insured was not liable;[23] or (4) capriciously refused to entertain a settlement offer with no regard given to the position of the insured.[24] The insurer is negligent in failing to settle if the ordinarily prudent insurer would consider that a decision to try the case created an unreasonable risk.[25] The insurer's liability for the entire judgment, including amounts in excess of policy limits, arises from the failure of

---

[20] *Southern General Ins. Co, v. Holt*, 262 Ga. 267, 268-69, 416 S.E.2d 274 (1992) (internal citations omitted).

[21] *Southern General Ins. Co. v. Holt*, 262 Ga. 267, 268-269, 416 S.E.2d 274 (1992); *Great American Ins. Co. v. Exum*, 123 Ga. App. 515, 519, 181 S.E.2d 704 (1971); *Cotton States Mut. Ins. Co. v. Phillips*, 110 Ga. App. 581, 584, 139 S.E.2d 412 (1964).

[22] *Southern General Ins. Co. v. Holt*, 262 Ga. 267, 268-69, 416 S.E.2d 274 (1992); *U.S. Fidelity & Guar. Co. v. Evans*, 116 Ga. App. 93, 156 S.E.2d 809 (1967).

[23] *U.S. Fid. & Guar. Co. v. Evans*, 116 Ga. App. 93, 95, 156 S.E.2d 809, 811 (1967) ("Thus, if the insurer refuses to settle a claim because it believes that the insured is not liable, it is nevertheless answerable for such refusal if its belief was arbitrary or capricious.").

[24] *Cotton States Mut. Ins. Co. v. Fields*, 106 Ga. App. 740, 741, 128 S.E.2d 358 (1962) (dictum).

[25] *Cotton States Mut. Ins. Co. v. Brightman*, 276 Ga. 683, 685, 580 S.E.2d 519, 521 (2003).

the insurer to exercise the proper standard of care in refusing to settle.[26]

§ 3.4   THE TIME-LIMITED *HOLT* DEMAND

The most common failure to settle within policy limits involves the insurer's rejection of a time-limited offer. A notable 1992 decision provides the moniker for the so-called "*Holt* demand," in which an attorney for a claimant sends a letter to the insurer demanding a settlement at or below policy limits and threatening the specter of a judgment in excess of policy limits if the demand is not accepted within a specified time period.[27] In *Holt*, the Supreme Court of Georgia addressed whether a demand letter providing the insurer 10 days to make a decision was sufficient.[28]

In upholding the rulings and verdict against the insurer, the Supreme Court limited its holding in two distinct ways: First, an insurance company does not act in bad faith solely because it fails to accept a settlement offer within the deadline set by the injured person's attorney.[29] Each claim is different, so the factors the insurer must consider in deciding whether to accept a settlement offer vary. The *Holt* court specifically mentioned three factors – the strength of the liability case against the insured, the risk to the insured of a judgment in excess of policy limits, and damages to which the claimant may be entitled under applicable tort law – that must also be considered when deciding on any opportunity to settle. Second, the Supreme Court stated that "[n]othing in this decision is intended to lay down a rule of law that would mean that a plaintiff's attorney under similar circumstances could 'set up' an insurer for an excess

---

[26]   *Nationwide Mut. Ins. Co. v. Turner*, 135 Ga. App. 551, 552, 218 S.E.2d 276 (1975); *Jones v. Southern Home Ins. Co.*, 135 Ga. App. 385, 388, 217 S.E.2d 620 (1975).

[27]   *Southern General Ins. Co, v. Holt*, 262 Ga. 267, 416 S.E.2d 274 (1992).

[28]   *Id.* 262 Ga. at 267.

[29]   *Id.* 262 Ga. at 269.

judgment merely by offering to settle within the policy limits and by imposing an unreasonably short time within which the offer would remain open."[30]

Thus, although the *Holt* court accepted a 10-day deadline for an insurer to accept an offer, *Holt* does not stand for the proposition that 10 days is appropriate in all situations. The length of the deadline depends on the facts and circumstances of the case at hand. For example, consider a simple car-wreck case where liability against the insured is reasonably clear, where the claimant has finished treating and sufficient medical expenses and lost wages can be documented and presented with the demand, and policy limits are at the statutory minimum. In such a case, 10 days should be sufficient for the insurer to analyze the documentation, make a decision as to the value of the case and prepare and deliver payment. In a case where the permanency of the claimant's injuries are still in doubt, and the available policy limits are substantially high in relation to the known damages, an insurer may reasonably require additional time or additional information to determine the reasonable likelihood that policy limits might be pierced.

Consistent with *Holt*, obvious "policy limits" claims justify a 10-day demand period. In claims that are not so obvious, or in which the insurer has not had a reasonable opportunity to investigate liability and damages, a time-limited demand might still be appropriate, but more time might be reasonably necessary for the insurer to digest the new information, conclude its independent investigation and respond to the offer to settle.

Other factual scenarios might create a situation where a reasonable insurer must respond to a demand to settle within policy limits in rather short order. For example, if the insurer is providing a defense, the parties go to media-

---

[30] *Id.* 262 Ga. at 269.

tion, and sufficient discovery has taken place to establish that there is a significant risk to the insured of a judgment in excess of policy limits, an insurer may have a matter of hours during the mediation to respond to a policy-limits demand. An even shorter deadline might reasonably occur during trial if a key witness fails to perform, performs better than expected, or other vagaries of trial create a significant risk to the insured of a judgment in excess of policy limits. In these situations, it is interesting to note that both parties are subject to the constraints of time. In the mediation scenario, the parties have the mediator and their respective clients' focused attention for an afternoon. In the trial scenario, the jury may be out deliberating with both parties evaluating the risk of an adverse decision.

Insurers sometimes ask for extensions to respond to time-limited demands. Any insurer requesting an extension should provide, and any claimant considering whether to grant an extension should request, a reasonably articulated explanation as to why an extension is needed, If the explanation is reasonably necessary, *Holt* would seem to suggest that failing to provide the extension would run afoul of the cautionary language in *Holt* warning against a claimant's attorney "set[ting] up an insurer for an excess judgment merely by offering to settle within the policy limits and by imposing an unreasonably short time within which the offer would remain open."[31]

In summary, because the test of the insurer's response to a time-limited demand is measured by the standard of the reasonably prudent insurer, the reasonableness of the terms of the demand is a central factor. Because the facts going to liability, damages and whether the insurer had a reasonable opportunity to settle vary widely from case to case, whether

---

[31] *Id.* 262 Ga. at 269.

the insurer was negligent or acted in bad faith is usually to be decided by a jury.[32]

§ 3.5   ACCEPTANCE AND REJECTION OF THE TIME-LIMITED DEMAND

The law of contract formation with respect to offers, counteroffers and rejections informs whether an insurer fails to take advantage of an offer to settle within policy limits.[33] Accordingly, when negotiating a possible settlement within policy limits, the following rules apply:

- The offeror is master of his offer and may condition the terms under which an offer may be accepted.[34]
- Failure to accept the offer in strict compliance with its terms or an "acceptance" that purports to vary a single term is deemed a rejection.[35]
- A counteroffer is a rejection of the initial offer.[36]

---

[32] "The jury generally must decide whether the insurer, *in view of the existing circumstances*, has accorded the insured the same faithful consideration it gives its own interest." *S. Gen. Ins. Co. v. Holt*, 262 Ga. 267, 268-69, 416 S.E.2d 274, 276 (1992) (emphasis added). "Georgia courts generally hold that the reasonableness of an insurer's response in a tortious failure to settle claim is a question for the jury." *Butler v. First Acceptance Ins. Co., Inc.*, 652 F. Supp. 2d 1264, 1277 (N.D. Ga. 2009) (denying summary judgment because a jury must decide "whether under *the totality of the circumstances* . . . Plaintiff can show that Defendant did not act as an ordinarily prudent insurer") (emphasis added). "[I]t is for the jury to decide whether the insurer has or has not so acted [in bad faith]." *Exum*, 123 Ga. App. at 519, 181 S.E.2d at 707.

[33] *See, e.g., Fortner v. Grange Mut. Ins. Co.*, 286 Ga. 189, 190-191, 686 S.E.2d 93 (2009) (noting that when insurer agrees to pay policy limits subject to conditions not part of the original demand, the claimant could consider the offer rejected).

[34] *Carterosa, Ltd. v. General Star Indem. Co.*, 227 Ga. App. 246, 248-249, 489 S.E.2d 83 (1997) ("the offeror may specify a method through which the offer must be accepted").

[35] *Herring v. Dunning*, 213 Ga. App. 695, 698, 446 S.E.2d 199 (1994), citing *Monk v. McDaniel*, 116 Ga. 108, 108(3), 42 S.E. 360 (1902) ("an answer to an offer will not amount to an acceptance, so as to result in a contract, unless it is unequivocal and identical with the terms of the offer"); *Lamb v. Decatur Fed. Sav. & Loan Ass'n*, 201 Ga. App. 583, 585, 411 S.E.2d 527, 529 (1991) ("[A] subsequent communication by one party to the alleged contract that varies even one term of the original offer is a counteroffer.").

- Oral agreements to settle are binding.[37]

In accordance with these rules of contract formation, a claimant may send a *Holt* demand to an insurer stating, for example, that the claimant will accept a certain amount so long as the insurer accepts the offer in writing by a certain date. If the insurer fails to respond within the stated time limit, the insurer has rejected the offer as a matter of law. If the insurer makes a counteroffer prior to the deadline, the insurer has rejected the offer as a matter of law. If the claimant rejects the insurer's counteroffer, the insurer may not then accept the original offer, even if within the originally stated time, unless the claimant revives the offer. Finally, such dealings may be consummated in writing, orally, or in any combination, though problems of proof may occur with regards to negotiations and agreements not confirmed in writing.

Whether or not an insurer has made a counteroffer to a time-limited demand has been hotly litigated in recent years. The Supreme Court of Georgia has consistently applied the age-old common-law rules of contract formation stated above to hold that a response by the insurance company that does "not purport to accept [the claimant's] offer unequivocally and without variance of any sort" is a rejection.[38] *Frickey v. Jones* is typical of these disputes in that it arises in the context of a motion to enforce settlement agreement. In *Frickey v. Jones*, the claimant sent a demand letter providing the insurer a five-day period to accept an

---

[36] *Duval & Co. v. Malcolm*, 233 Ga. 784, 787, 214 S.E.2d 356 (1975) ("a counter-offer operates to reject the offer and terminate the power of acceptance"); *Lamb v. Decatur Fed. Sav. & Loan Ass'n*, 201 Ga. App. 583, 585, 411 S.E.2d 527, 529 (1991) ("A proposal to accept, or an acceptance, upon terms varying from those offered, is a rejection of the offer, and puts an end to the negotiation.").

[37] *Poulous v. Home Federal Sav. & Loan Ass'n*, 192 Ga. App. 501, 502, 385 S.E.2d 135 (1989), citing *Mason v. Rabun Waste*, 174 Ga. App. 462, 463, 330 S.E.2d 400 (1985) ("Under Georgia law, a definite, certain and unambiguous oral contract of settlement of a pending cause of action is a valid and binding agreement.").

[38] *Frickey v. Jones*, 280 Ga. 573, 575, 630 S.E.2d 374, 376 (2006).

offer to settle for policy limits.[39] The insurer responded within the five-day period, stating its willingness to tender policy limits and as follows: "Obviously, payment is complicated by what appears to be a Grady Hospital lien as well as potential liens by your client's health carrier. Please advise me of the status of these liens."[40]

The claimant viewed this language as a rejection of the demand under the theory that it added the condition of resolving liens prior to payment. The insurer agreed, later writing that it would "tender the policy limits . . . *if you were able to resolve the Grady Hospital lien as well as potential liens by your client's health carriers."*[41] The insurer, on behalf of its insured, filed a motion to enforce the alleged settlement agreement. The Supreme Court of Georgia ruled that no settlement agreement had been made, as the insurer purported to "accept" the offer on the condition that liens be resolved, making the attempted acceptance a counteroffer.[42]

The Supreme Court of Georgia again addressed a nearly identical exchange in *McReynolds v. Krebs.*[43] In *McReynolds v. Krebs*, the claimant made a time-limited demand for policy limits that did not mention how a known lien by Grady Hospital would be resolved. The insurer made a timely response as follows:

> Our limits are $25,000/$50,000 and we agree to settle this matter for the $25,000 per person limit. Please

---

[39] Although the Court in *Frickey v. Jones* made no rulings with regard to bad faith and the reasonableness of the demand, the five-day time period does not appear to be problematic. The five-day deadline was simply to manifest an acceptance of the offer with no requirement that payment actually be tendered within the five-day period. Also, the insurer had manifested a desire to pay the limits prior to the five-day demand. 280 Ga. 573, 573, 630 S.E.2d 374, 375.

[40] 280 Ga. 573, 573, 630 S.E.2d 374, 375.

[41] *Frickey v. Jones*, 280 Ga. 573, 574, 630 S.E.2d 374, 376 (2006).

[42] *See also, Fortner v. Grange Mut. Ins. Co.*, 286 Ga. 189, 686 S.E.2d 93 (2009) (noting that response to demand that added additional conditions was a counteroffer that did not entitle insurer to "safe harbor" from bad faith).

[43] 290 Ga. 850, 725 S.E.2d 584 (2012).

call me in order to discuss how the lien(s) (Specifically, but not limited to the $273,435.35 lien from
Grady Memorial Hospital) will be resolved as part of
this settlement.[44]

In the motion to enforce settlement that followed, the insurer argued that its reference to the lien merely made an
inquiry and did not add conditions to the demand. The Supreme Court disagreed, noting that the language used did
not inquire as to the existence of liens but indicated that
counsel needed to discuss how the known liens would be resolved as part of the settlement. Accordingly, a counteroffer
was made.[45]

The issue of whether a counteroffer was made arises in many
bad-faith cases, as insurers sometimes defend such cases on
the theory that it had accepted an offer to settle within policy
limits that the claimant refused to consummate.[46]

§ 3.6   "OPPORTUNITY" TO SETTLE WITHIN POLICY LIMITS

The common occurrence of a written *Holt* demand notwithstanding, there is no requirement under Georgia law that
the insurer's failure to settle within policy limits be proven
by the insurer's failure to accept a formal, written demand
within a stated time. Rather, the law requires an inquiry
into "whether the insurer had an *opportunity* to make an
effective compromise."[47] Although refusing to place an "affirmative duty on the company to engage in negotiations
concerning a settlement demand that is *in excess* of the in-

---

[44]   290 Ga. at 853, 725 S.E.2d at 588.

[45]   *See also, Torres v. Elkin*, 317 Ga. App. 135, 142, 730 S.E.2d 518, 524
(2012) (ruling that language stating, "I trust that your office will satisfy any liens
arising out of this matter," is sufficiently insistent to indicate a requirement for
the insurer's acceptance to be effective, making it a counteroffer).

[46]   *Butler v. First Acceptance Ins. Co., Inc.*, 652 F. Supp. 2d 1264, 1277
(N.D. Ga. 2009) (relying on *Frickey* to rule that an insurance company rejects a
time-limited demand by making a counteroffer).

[47]   *Cotton States Mut. Ins. Co. v. Brightman*, 276 Ga. 683, 685, 580 S.E.2d
519 (2003) (emphasis added).

surance policy's limits,"[48] the Georgia Supreme Court has not required that the "opportunity to make an effective compromise" be in any particular form.

The "argument that an insurer may not be held liable for tortious refusal to settle in the absence of a settlement demand from the plaintiff is not supported by Georgia law."[49] Indeed, the Georgia Court of Appeals has held that in the appropriate situation an insurer may have a duty to make an offer: "The failure either to settle within policy limits *or to make an offer of settlement* creates an issue of bad faith of the insurer, because the issue arises whether the insurer places its financial interest superior to the interests of its insured who is placed at great risk for an excess judgment."[50]

The Northern District of Georgia, applying its understanding of Georgia law, has ruled that there is no bad faith as a matter of law unless "the case could have been settled within the policy limits-and that the insurer knew, or reasonably should have known, of this fact."[51]   In *Kingsely v. State Farm*, "[p]rior to filing suit, neither [claimant] nor her attorneys made a settlement demand or requested to discuss settlement with State Farm."[52]   State Farm tendered policy limits within a month of suit being filed. The claimant rejected the tender and proceeded to obtain a verdict in excess of policy limits. In the subsequent bad-faith lawsuit, the claimant acknowledged that she had made no demand and testified that she had decided to obtain an excess judgment if State Farm did not offer its limits prior to her deadline for filing a lawsuit. The deadline for filing a lawsuit was not communicated to State Farm. The court ruled that there

[48]   *Id*. 276 Ga. at 685.
[49]   *Kingsley v. State Farm Mut. Auto Ins. Co.*, 353 F. Supp. 2d 1242, 1252 (N.D. Ga. 2005), *aff'd*, 153 F. App'x 555 (11th Cir. 2005).
[50]   *Thomas*, 253 Ga. App. at 204-05, 558 S.E.2d at 439 (emphasis added).
[51]   *Kingsley v. State Farm Mut. Auto. Ins. Co.*, 353 F. Supp. 2d 1242, 1248 (N.D. Ga. 2005) *aff'd*, 153 F. App'x 555 (11th Cir. 2005).
[52]   353 F. Supp. 2d at 1243.

was no bad faith as a matter of law, as State Farm had no knowledge of the claimant's "secret deadline" and that there was no evidence that State Farm knew of any "triggering event" alerting State Farm to an opportunity to settle.[53]

Thus, although the formal demand is highly useful as documentary proof of the insurer's failure to fulfill its duty, the demand itself may not be a necessary element of the tort. Rather, the necessary element is failure to take advantage of an opportunity to settle within policy limits. Although in the vast majority of bad-faith cases the opportunity is delivered to the insurer in the form of a written demand, in the appropriate case, an insurance company may have a reasonable opportunity to effect settlement and protect its insured from legal liability before any demand is sent. This opportunity could arise while the insurer fulfills its duties of investigating the claims against its insured.

PRACTICE POINTER: Whether a necessary element of the tort of bad faith or not, a formal, time-limited demand is a useful and sometimes necessary tool in getting a claim paid promptly. A for-profit entity like an insurance company is likely to avoid or delay payment unless prodded. A demand should be in writing and give the insurer sufficient information (in the form of medical invoices, statements of lost income, etc.) justifying the amount of the demand. The demand should clearly state the deadline and means of acceptance, with the amount of time being reasonably sufficient in the circumstances of the particular case. Send the demand via certified mail, return receipt requested, to insure a record of when the insurer received the letter. If the rejection of a reasonable offer is at mediation and possibly subject to confidentiality, consider following up with a formal letter making a demand that follows the suggestions above.

---

[53]   353 F. Supp. 2d at 1252-53.

§3.7   LEGISLATION REGARDING SOME OFFERS

As this edition went to press, the Governor signed a 2013 statute addressing certain offers to settle tort claims arising out of automobile accidents before a lawsuit is filed when those offers are made by claimants represented by counsel. The law will be codified at O.C.G.A. § 9-11-67.1, and reads as follows:

(a) Prior to the filing of a civil action, any offer to settle a tort claim for personal injury, bodily injury, or death arising from the use of a motor vehicle and prepared by or with the assistance of an attorney on behalf of a claimant or claimants shall be in writing and contain the following material terms:

   (1) The time period within which such offer must be accepted, which shall be not less than 30 days from receipt of the offer;

   (2) Amount of monetary payment;

   (3) The party or parties the claimant or claimants will release if such offer is accepted;

   (4) The type of release, if any, the claimant or claimants will provide to each releasee; and

   (5) The claims to be released.

(b) The recipients of an offer to settle made under this Code section may accept the same by providing written acceptance of the material terms outlined in subsection (a) of this Code section in their entirety.

(c) Nothing in this Code section is intended to prohibit parties from reaching a settlement agreement in a manner and under terms otherwise agreeable to the parties.

(d) Upon receipt of an offer to settle set forth in subsection (a) of this Code section, the recipients shall have the right to seek clarification regarding terms, liens, subrogation claims, standing to release claims, medical bills, medical records, and other relevant facts.

An attempt to seek reasonable clarification shall not be deemed a counteroffer.

(e) An offer to settle made pursuant to this Code section shall be sent by certified mail or statutory overnight delivery, return receipt requested, and shall specifically reference this Code section.

(f) The person or entity providing payment to satisfy the material term set forth in paragraph (2) of subsection (a) of this Code section may elect to provide payment by any one or more of the following means:

  (1) Cash;

  (2) Money order;

  (3) Wire transfer;

  (4) A cashier's check issued by a bank or other financial institution;

  (5) A draft or bank check issued by an insurance company; or

  (6) Electronic funds transfer or other method of electronic payment.

(g) Nothing in this Code section shall prohibit a party making an offer to settle from requiring payment within a specified period; provided, however, that such period shall be not less than ten days after the written acceptance of the offer to settle.

(h) This Code section shall apply to causes of action for personal injury, bodily injury, and death arising from the use of a motor vehicle on or after July 1, 2013.

The statute arose out of a perceived need by insurance companies to have additional time to respond to time-limited demands before a lawsuit is initiated and, presumably, before defense counsel is involved. When a claimant chooses to avail itself of the procedure outlined in the statute, the insurer will have at least 30 days to accept or reject the offer and an additional 10 days to finalize payment.

Notably, the statute does not mention "bad faith" or otherwise refer to the common law tort described in *Smoot*[54] and *Holt*.[55] Because this new statute's effective date (July 1, 2013) follows the printing of this edition, how courts will interpret and how claimants and insurers will utilize this procedure remains to be seen.

§ 3.8   "SAFE HARBOR" WHEN CERTAIN LIENS INVOLVED

The Georgia Court of Appeals has recently created a "safe harbor" for an insurer presented with an opportunity to settle a claim that involves certain healthcare liens. *S. Gen. Ins. Co. v. Wellstar Health Sys., Inc.*, provides a typical example of the manner in which a hospital lien could complicate efforts between the claimant and the insurer to settle claims against the insured.[56] In *Wellstar*, the insured injured a bicyclist. The insured's liability limits were insufficient to compensate the bicyclist for his damages. A healthcare provider (Wellstar) asserted a lien. The bicyclist accepted policy limits to settle the tort claim against the insured but would not agree to indemnify the insurer. The insurer paid the claimant anyway.

The healthcare provider succeeded in enforcing the lien against the insurer in the trial court. The insurer appealed, arguing that the familiar law of offers and counteroffers as applied in *Frickey v. Jones* conflicted with the potential liability to settling parties arising out of hospital lien law. Although declining to find any such conflict, the court in *Wellstar* created a "safe harbor" for insurers in the situation in which Southern General found itself, which was described as follows:

---

    [54] *See supra* §3.2 for a discussion of *Smoot v. State Farm Mut. Auto. Ins. Co.*, 299 F.2d 525 (5th Cir. 1962) ("Smoot I"); 337 F.2d 223 (5th Cir. 1964) ("Smoot II"); 381 F.2d 331 (5th Cir. 1967) ("Smoot III").
    [55] *See supra* §3.4 for a discussion of *Southern General Ins. Co, v. Holt*, 262 Ga. 267, 416 S.E.2d 274 (1992).
    [56] 315 Ga. App. 26, 726 S.E.2d 488 (2012).

> [I]t is possible for an insurance company to cre-
> ate a 'safe harbor' from liability under *Holt* and
> its progeny when (1) the insurer promptly acts
> to settle a case involving clear liability and
> special damages in excess of the applicable pol-
> icy limits, and (2) the *sole* reason for the par-
> ties' inability to reach a settlement is the
> plaintiff's unreasonable refusal to assure the
> satisfaction of any outstanding hospital liens.[57]

The court further explained its holding with the following
hypothetical:

> Consider the following hypothetical: An insur-
> ance company – faced with a situation of clear
> liability and special damages in excess of the
> policy limits – offers in a timely fashion to ten-
> der its policy limits to the plaintiff, *subject to a
> reasonably and narrowly tailored provision* as-
> suring that the plaintiff will satisfy any hospi-
> tal liens from the proceeds of such settlement
> payment. For example, the insurance com-
> pany could request that plaintiff's counsel or a
> third party hold a portion of the settlement
> proceeds (in an amount equal to that of the
> hospital lien) in escrow to allow the plaintiff an
> opportunity to investigate the validity of the
> liens and to negotiate with the hospital. And
> once the relevant lien-resolving documents
> have been executed by the parties, the held-
> back settlement funds could then be disbursed
> to the plaintiff. But if the insurer made such
> an offer or counteroffer (in a timely and rea-
> sonable fashion) and the plaintiff unreasonably
> refused to give the requested assurance, the

---

[57]   315 Ga. App. 26, 31, 726 S.E.2d 488, 493 (2012) (emphasis in original).

insurer is (at that point) under no obligation to tender policy limits directly to the plaintiff. Indeed, a plaintiff who unreasonably refuses to give such an assurance does so at his or her own peril because the insurance company would thereafter have no obligation to negotiate with the hospital or otherwise advocate on the plaintiff's behalf. *Instead, the insurer would be free (at that point) to simply verify the validity of any liens, make payment directly to the hospital, and then disburse any remaining funds to the plaintiff.*[58]

Most fundamentally, there was no bad faith in *Wellstar* and no allegations of bad faith. Indeed, there could be no bad faith because the insurer effectively settled the claims against its insured. Thus, the insured's interests and perspectives were not represented in the briefing and argument leading to the *Wellstar* decision. The only two interests represented, insurance companies and hospitals, can derive benefits from a "safe harbor" that allows the insurance company to pay the hospital without protecting the insured from legal liability. For that reason, any application of the safe harbor in a situation where there has actually been an excess judgment against the insured remains uncertain.

Wellstar is perhaps better viewed (and more easily reconciled) in relation to the reasonableness of the opportunity to settle and the actions of the reasonably prudent insurer in responding to such an opportunity. It would seem unrea-

---

[58]   315 Ga. App. 26, 32-33, 726 S.E.2d 488, 493 (2012) (emphasis added). The Court tempered its suggestion by noting as follows: "The hypothetical posited *supra* should in no way be read as condoning or encouraging an insurance company to make payment directly to a hospital before engaging in good-faith settlement negotiations with a plaintiff. And while we leave the answer to this question for another day, it is possible that an insurer would be liable under *Holt* and its progeny if the company made payment directly to the hospital before even attempting to negotiate with the plaintiff." *Id.* at FN 21.

sonable to fault an insurer for considering the effect of known and perfected liens when evaluating an opportunity to settle. However, a reasonably prudent insurer, giving equal consideration to the interests of its insured, should weigh the risk to the insured created by the lien as against the risk to the insured created by the legal liability to the claimant. *Wellstar* does not recognize or address those concerns, arguably making it contrary to existing authority.[59]

§ 3.9 DAMAGES

Although an insurer's failure to defend a covered claim is a breach of the insurance contract, a claim for bad faith refusal to settle within policy limits sounds in tort, not contract.[60] Like any tort, damages are an essential element to a claim for bad faith. Since the *Smoot* cases, Georgia law has recognized several categories of available damages: (1) special damages; (2) general damages; (3) punitive damages; and (3) attorneys' fees.[61]

§ 3.10 SPECIAL DAMAGES

Special damages consist of the judgment against the insured that the insurer refuses to pay. In the typical case, where the insurer has tendered limits but refuses to pay amounts in excess of limits after having allowed a judgment to be entered, the special damages are the difference between policy limits and the amount in excess of policy limits. In cases where the insurer is refusing to pay anything, perhaps because of a purported coverage defense, special damages would be the entire judgment. Where an insurance company fails to offer a defense, it may be liable to its insured beyond

---

[59] *See Fortner v. Grange Mut. Ins. Co.*, 286 Ga. 189, 190 (2009) (acknowledging that Georgia follows "equal consideration rule").

[60] *McCall v. Allstate Ins. Co.*, 251 Ga. 869, 870, 310 S.E.2d 513 (1984); *Alexander Underwriters Gen. Agency v. Lovett*, 182 Ga. App. 769, 772-773, 357 S.E.2d 258 (1987).

[61] *Smoot v. State Farm Mut. Auto. Ins. Co.*, 381 F.2d 331, 341 (5th Cir. 1967) ("Smoot III").

the policy limits to the full amount of the judgment.[62] An insurer who is liable for bad faith may be liable for the full amount of the judgment, even in excess of the policy limits, where the consequential damages can be traced directly to the failure to timely defend or settle.[63] The issue of whether the insured is entitled to judgment in excess of the policy limits is a matter for the jury.[64] An insurer may be liable to its insured for post-judgment interest that the insured is required to pay.[65]

In addition, if the insured incurred legal fees in its own defense (for example, when the insurer refused to defend its insured), such legal fees are recoverable as special damages.[66]

§ 3.11 GENERAL DAMAGES

General damages are of the type typically found in tort cases and caused by the tortfeasor's negligence or bad faith. For example, in *Smoot III*, the judgment in excess of policy limits caused a foreclosure and ruined the insured's credit, jus-

---

[62] *Atlanta Cas. Ins. Co. v. Gardenhire*, 248 Ga. App. 42, 44, 545 S.E.2d 182 (2001), citing *Leader Nat. Ins. Co. v. Kemp & Son, Inc.*, 259 Ga. 329, 330, 380 S.E.2d 458 (1989) and *Leader Nat. Ins. Co. v. Smith*, 177 Ga. App. 267, 278-279, 339 S.E.2d 321 (1985).

[63] *Thomas v. Atlanta Cas. Co.*, 253 Ga. App. 199, 204, 558 S.E.2d 432 (2001).

[64] *Id*. 253 Ga. App. at 204; *Leader Nat. Ins. Co. v. Kemp & Son, Inc.*, 259 Ga. 329, 330, 380 S.E.2d 458 (1989); *Atlanta Cas. Ins. Co. v. Gardenhire*, 248 Ga. App. 42, 44, 545 S.E.2d 182 (2001) ("[W]here an insurance company fails to offer a defense, it may be liable to its insured beyond the policy limits to the full amount of the judgment ... a jury question exists as to the extent of its liability).

[65] *Hulsey v. The Travelers Indemnity Company of America*, 460 F. Supp. 2d 1332, 1337-1338 (N.D. Ga. 2006) (noting that *Southern General Ins Co v. Ross*, 227 Ga. App. 191, 489 S.E.2d 53 (1997), did not hold that the duty to pay interest abates when an insurer tenders its policy limits).

[66] *Rutledge v. Dixie Auto. Ins. Co.*, 106 Ga. App. 577, 579, 127 S.E.2d 683, 685 (1962) ("[I]t is settled in this State that when an insurer wrongfully denies coverage to its insured, the latter may settle his liability without litigation and without the insurer's consent, the insurance company being bound to reimburse the insured in the amount of any settlement made in good faith plus expenses and attorneys' fees.").

tifying $10,000 in general damages.[67] Other proof of such damages may, in the proper case and with appropriate proof, include exposure to post-judgment discovery and collection efforts, damage to reputation or business interests caused by a judgment of record, or various types of mental or psychological injury.

§ 3.12 PUNITIVE DAMAGES

When an insurer fails to settle claims against its insured within policy limits when it has a reasonable opportunity to do so, the insurer may be subject to punitive damages.[68] An insurer's failure to take advantage of a single, time-limited demand for policy limits can create a jury question as to punitive damages.[69] Even without the existence of an express, time-limited demand from the claimant, there may be a jury issue as to punitive damages when there is a fact issue as to whether the insurer should have *initiated* settlement discussions.[70]

Whether an insurer's bad faith subjects it to punitive damages is governed by the familiar standards applicable to other torts and set forth in O.C.G.A. § 51-12-5.1.[71] Under that statute, punitive damages may be awarded only when it is proven by "clear and convincing evidence" that the defendant's actions showed "willful misconduct, malice, fraud, wantonness, oppression, or that entire want of care which would raise the presumption of conscious indifference to con-

---

[67] *Smoot v. State Farm Mut. Auto. Ins. Co.*, 381 F.2d 331, 338 (5th Cir. 1967).

[68] *Thomas v. Atlanta Cas. Co.*, 253 Ga. App. 199, 205, 558 S.E.2d 432 (2001).

[69] *Southern General Ins. Co. v. Holt*, 262 Ga. 267, 416 S.E.2d 274 (1992) (acknowledging appropriateness of punitive damages in bad faith cases).

[70] *Whiteside v. Infinity Cas. Ins. Co.*, 2008 WL 3456508 (M.D. Ga.) (denying insurer's motion for summary judgment on punitive damages).

[71] *Thomas v. Atlanta Cas. Co.*, 253 Ga. App. 199, 205, 558 S.E.2d 432 (2001) ("Where there has been such entire want of care amounting to a conscious indifference to the consequences . . . this creates a jury question as to whether clear and convincing evidence exists as to such conduct.").

sequences."[72]   If punitive damages are awarded, they are generally capped at $250,000.[73] The cap does not apply, and a jury may award unlimited punitive damages, upon a finding that the defendant had "specific intent to cause harm."[74] Because O.C.G.A. § 51-12-5.1 has general applicability, judicial construction of the statute in cases other than those involving an insurer's bad faith failure to settle is highly relevant.

(a)   Entitlement to punitive damages up to $250,000.

"Willful misconduct," as used by the courts in authorizing punitive damages, is generally defined as the conscious or intentional disregard of the rights of another.[75] The term "conscious indifference to the consequences" has been defined as the "[i]ntentional disregard of the rights of another, knowingly or willfully disregarding such rights."[76] It is not essential to a recovery for punitive damages that the person inflicting the damages was guilty of willful and intentional misconduct, if the act was done under such circumstances as evinces an entire want of care and a conscious indifference to the consequences.[77]

The fact that many victims of an insurance company's bad faith do not always suffer direct personal injury does not remove the potential for punitive damages. Nor is it relevant that there might be no personal contact between the insured and the insurance company adjuster that decides not to settle within policy limits. This is because neither direct personal contact nor specific malice between the de-

---

[72]   O.C.G.A. § 51-12-5.1(b).
[73]   O.C.G.A. § 51-12-5.1(g).
[74]   O.C.G.A. § 51-12-5.1(f).
[75]   *Investment Securities Corp. v. Cole*, 186 Ga. 809, 109 S.E. 126 (1938).
[76]   *Wardlaw v. Ivey*, 297 Ga. App. 240, 676 S.E.2d 858 (2009).
[77]   *Hodges v. Effingham County Hosp. Auth.*, 182 Ga. App. 173, 355 S.E.2d 104 (1987).

fendant and plaintiff is required to support a claim for punitive damages.[78] In *Bowen v. Waters*, an automobile owner sued a store for property damage to his automobile. The damage occurred when the automobile was forced off the road by a store employee who was following the automobile because he suspected the driver of shoplifting. Because there was evidence that the defendant's acts were done with reckless disregard or with a conscious indifference to the rights of the plaintiff, the court ruled that there was a fact issue as to punitive damages.

Entitlement to punitive damages must be proven by clear and convincing evidence.[79] A jury may award punitive damages even where the clear and convincing evidence only creates an inference of the defendant's conscious indifference to the consequences of his acts.[80]

Specific to bad-faith cases, "conscious indifference to the consequences" may be shown where an adjuster who is in possession of a time-limited demand, knowing the insured is 100 percent liable and knowing that "special" damages already exceeded policy limits, fails to accept the offer within the deadline or ask for an extension.[81] Also, once it has been determined that the insurer tortiously refused to accept an offer within policy limits (and the issue of punitive damages does not come up until that underlying issue is decided), the insurer has "gamble[d] with the funds of its insured"[82] and failed to give its insured's interests "equal consideration,"[83] violating duties in Georgia law long-known to all liability

---

[78] *Bowen v. Waters*, 170 Ga. App. 65, 67, 316 S.E.2d 497 (1984), *cert. denied*, April 6, 1984.

[79] O.C.G.A. § 51-12-5.1(b).

[80] *Tookes v. Murray*, 297 Ga. App. 765, 768, 678 S.E.2d 209 (2009), citing *Mr. Transmission, Inc. v. Thompson*, 173 Ga. App. 773, 775, 328 S.E.2d 397 (1985).

[81] *Dickerson v. Am. Nat'l Property and Ca. Co.*, 2009 WL 1035131, *10 (M.D. Ga.).

[82] *McCall v. Allstate Ins. Co.*, 251 Ga. 869, 870, 310 S.E.2d 513 (1984).

[83] *Fortner v. Grange Mut. Ins. Co.*, 286 Ga. 189, 190 (2009).

insurers. Indeed, an insurer who undertakes the defense of an insured under a liability policy has established a fiduciary relationship.[84] Thus, it is difficult for the insurer to claim that its failure was of the type of "mere negligence" that will not support a claim for punitive damages.

(b)   Entitlement to more than $250,000 in punitive damages.

The statutory cap of $250,000 on punitive damages is lifted where the trier of fact finds that the defendant acted, or failed to act, with "specific intent to cause harm."[85]

A party possesses specific intent to cause harm when that party desires to cause the consequences of its act *or* believes that the consequences are substantially certain to result from it. *Intent is always a question for the jury.* It may be shown by direct or circumstantial evidence.[86]

Whether the defendant acted or failed to act with the specific intent to cause harm is determined by the common law standard of preponderance of the evidence.[87]

---

[84]   *United States Fidelity & Guar. Co. v. Evans*, 116 Ga. App. 93, 95, 156 S.E.2d 809, 811 (1967), *aff'd.*, 223 Ga. 789 (1967) ("It is not sufficient for the insurer to consult its own self-interest. As a professional in the defense of suits, it must use a degree of skill commensurate with such professional standards. . . . Its relationship is somewhat of a fiduciary one."); and *Delancy v. St. Paul Fire & Marine Ins. Co.*, 947 F. 2d 1536, 1545-46 (11th Cir. 1991) (recognizing that contractual relationship between insured and liability insurer creates an "independent duty" supporting an action in tort when the insurer's negligent refusal to settle a claim causes damage to the insured not otherwise covered by the insurance contract).

[85]   *Brewer v. Insight Technology Inc.*, 2009 WL 4263771, *4 (Ga. App. 2009) (affirming finding of specific intent to cause harm and punitive damages in excess of statutory cap); and *Rolleston v. Estate of Sims*, 253 Ga. App. 182 (2001) (affirming award of punitive damages in excess of $250,000 for allegations of fraudulent conveyance).

[86]   *Ga. Pattern Jury Instructions*, Civ. 66.711 (emphasis added).

[87]   *Kothari v. Patel*, 262 Ga. App. 168, 173-174, 585 S.E.2d 97 (2003).

It is hard to imagine a situation where the issue of whether the insurer acted with specific intent to cause harm would *not* be a jury question. As noted, a liability insurer who declines a reasonable opportunity to protect its insured has breached its fiduciary duty to the insured.[88] Thus, the insurer specifically knows who will be harmed by any failure to settle. Moreover, the decision to not settle or defend is rarely made by accident. Discovery of the claims file will usually show the deliberativeness of the process of making such decisions, highlighting the "intent" of the act.

(c)   Other issues regarding punitive damages.

The question of whether to impose punitive damages is for the trier of fact.[89] Whether the tort was sufficiently aggravating to authorize punitive damages is a jury question.[90] Punitive damages are not compensation for injury to a plaintiff, but are private fines levied by civil juries to punish reprehensible conduct and to deter its future occurrence.[91] A deterrence award is based on factors, for the most part, unrelated to the injury to any particular victim, and is limited only by the collective conscience of the jury.[92]

---

[88]   *United States Fidelity & Guar. Co. v. Evans*, 116 Ga. App. 93, 95, 156 S.E.2d 809, 811 (1967), *aff'd.*, 223 Ga. 789 (1967) ("It is not sufficient for the insurer to consult its own self-interest. As a professional in the defense of suits, it must use a degree of skill commensurate with such professional standards. . . . Its relationship is somewhat of a fiduciary one."); and *Delancy v. St. Paul Fire & Marine Ins. Co.*, 947 F. 2d 1536, 1545-46 (11th Cir. 1991) (recognizing that contractual relationship between insured and liability insurer creates an "independent duty" supporting an action in tort when the insurer's negligent refusal to settle a claim causes damage to the insured not otherwise covered by the insurance contract).

[89]   *Covington Square Associates, LLC v. Ingles Markets, Inc.*, 300 Ga. App. 740, 745, 686 S.E.2d 359 (2009), citing *Morales v. Webb*, 200 Ga. App. 788, 790, 409 S.E.2d 572 (1991); *Petrolane Gas Svc. v. Eusery*, 193 Ga. App. 860, 862, 389 S.E.2d 355 (1989).

[90]   *Tookes v. Murray*, 297 Ga. App. 765, 768, 678 S.E.2d 209 (2009), citing *Mr. Transmission, Inc. v. Thompson*, 173 Ga. App. 773, 775, 328 S.E.2d 397 (1985).

[91]   O.C.G.A. § 51-12-5.1(c).

[92]   *Southeastern Security Insurance Co. v. Hotle*, 222 Ga. App. 161 (1996).

Punitive damages may not be recovered where there is no entitlement to compensatory damages.[93] A claim for punitive damages may not be assigned.[94] Thus, when an insured assigns tort claims for bad faith or negligent refusal to settle to a third party, the insured forfeits the right to recover punitive damages based on those claims.[95] Punitive damages must be specifically prayed for in a complaint.[96]

§ 3.13 ATTORNEYS' FEES

Expenses of litigation under O.C.G.A. § 13-6-11 may be allowed in common law bad faith claims against an insurer.[97]

§ 3.14 ASSIGNMENTS, CONSENT JUDGMENTS AND *DOWSE* SETTLEMENTS

Many lawsuits involving an insurer's bad-faith failure to settle are brought by the claimant and not by the insured. Others are brought by both the claimant and the insured. Because a third-party claimant that lacks privity with the insurance company generally has no cause of action against the insurer for claims handling,[98] a claimant who prosecutes

---

[93] *Southern General Ins. Co. v. Holt*, 262 Ga. 267, 269, 416 S.E.2d 274 (1992), citing *Barnes v. White County Bank*, 170 Ga. App. 681, 318 S.E.2d 74 (1984).

[94] *Canal Indem. Co. v. Greene*, 265 Ga. App. 67, 72, 593 S.E.2d 41 (2003), citing *Southern R. Co. v. Malone Freight Lines*, 174 Ga. App. 405, 408-409, 330 S.E.2d 371 (1985) and *In Re Estate of Sims*, 259 Ga. App. 786, 791 n.2, 578 S.E.2d 498 (2003). *See also Empire Fire & Marine Ins. Co. v. Driskell*, 264 Ga. App. 646, 649, 592 S.E.2d 80 (2003).

[95] *Southern General Ins. Co. v. Holt*, 262 Ga. 267, 269, 416 S.E.2d 274 (1992).

[96] O.C.G.A. § 51-12-5.1(d)(1). *See Drug Emporium, Inc. v. Peaks*, 227 Ga. App. 121, 126-127, 488 S.E.2d 500 (1997) (claimant not entitled to punitive damages against remaining defendant where claimant only prayed for punitive damages against co-defendant who was dismissed from case).

[97] *Alexander Underwriters Gen. Agency v. Lovett*, 182 Ga. App. 769, 772-773(2), 357 S.E.2d 258 (1987).

[98] *But see*, O.C.G.A. § 33-6-7, discussed at § 2.10, *infra.*, creating a cause of action for claimants whose property damage claims are handled in bad faith by a tortfeasor's automobile liability carrier.

a bad-faith claim generally does so by taking an assignment from the insured. Because liability policies have clauses forbidding the insured from assigning claims or settling claims without the insurer's consent, such assignments can only be accomplished in certain situations.

The classic situation was presented in *Southern Guaranty Ins. Co. v. Dowse.*[99] In that case, the claimant brought a lawsuit against a contractor who was insured under a commercial general liability policy. The insurer denied coverage and refused to defend. The claimant and insured entered into a settlement agreement, under which the insured withdrew its answer and allowed a default judgment to be rendered against it. The settlement agreement also provided that the claimant would not seek to enforce the judgment against the insured's personal assets, but would limit its recovery to any amounts due under the insurance policy. The matter went to trial on damages. Damages were awarded against the insured, and the claimant initiated a garnishment action directly against the contractor's insurance company.

The insurer argued that because the insured faced no liability under the settlement agreement, there was no indemnity obligation for the insurer to undertake. The insurer also argued that it was relieved of liability because the insured had breached policy provisions barring settlement without the insurer's consent. The Supreme Court of Georgia rejected both defenses, holding that an insurer that refuses to defend based upon a belief that a claim against its insured is excluded from a policy's scope of coverage "[does] so at its peril, and if the insurer guesses wrong, it must bear the consequences, legal or otherwise, of its breach of contract."[100] The Court continued as follows:

---

[99] *Southern Guar. Ins. Co. v. Dowse*, 278 Ga. 674, 605 S.E.2d 27 (2004).
[100] *Id.* 278 Ga. at 676.

In Georgia, an insurer that denies coverage and refuses to defend an action against its insured, when it
could have done so with a reservation of its rights as
to coverage, waives the provisions of the policy
against a settlement by the insured and becomes
bound to pay the amount of any settlement within a
policy's limits made in good faith, plus expenses and
attorneys' fees.[101]

Similarly, an insurer who denies coverage waives the provisions (common in most liability policies) barring coverage
when the insured has made "voluntary payment" to the
claimant.[102] Furthermore, if an insurer refuses to defend a
third-party action against its insured after timely notice, the
insurer is bound to the issues adjudicated in the underlying
suit against its insured.[103] If the insurer is then sued for the
refusal to defend or failure to pay a judgment entered
against the insured, the insurer may not relitigate issues
that form the basis for the judgment entered against its insured.[104] However, an insurer's refusal to defend does not
waive its right to contest whether the insurance policy provides coverage for the underlying claim.[105]

The insured may not unilaterally settle a lawsuit, however,
if the insurer is defending the insured in the lawsuit but refuses to settle the lawsuit within policy limits.[106] In *Trinity*

---

[101]   *Id.* 278 Ga. at 676.
[102]   *Owners Ins. Co. v. Smith Mechanical Contractors, Inc.*, 285 Ga. 807,
683 S.E.2d 599 (2009) (affirming judgment for insured who voluntarily paid for
the replacement of equipment damaged by the insured after the insurer denied
coverage).
[103]   *Atlanta Cas. Ins. Co. v. Gardenhire*, 248 Ga. App. 42, 44, 545 S.E.2d
182 (2001).
[104]   *Id.; see also Morgan v. Guaranty National Cos.*, 268 Ga. 343, 489
S.E.2d 803 (1997).
[105]   *Southern Guar. Ins. Co. v. Dowse*, 278 Ga. 674, 676, 605 S.E.2d 27, 29
(2004), citing *Aetna Cas. & Surety Co. v. Empire Fire & Marine Ins. Co.*, 212 Ga.
App. 642, 646, 442 S.E.2d 778 (1994); *McCraney v. Fire & Cas. Ins. Co.*, 182 Ga.
App. 895, 896, 357 S.E.2d 327 (1987).
[106]   *Trinity Outdoor, LLC. v. Central Mut. Ins. Co.*, 285 Ga. 583, 679
S.E.2d 10 (2009).

Outdoor, LLC. v. Central Mut. Ins. Co., a billboard fell while it was being installed on Trinity's property, killing two persons. Investigations ultimately determined that the manufacturer of the billboard was primarily at fault, though liability for Trinity could not be ruled out. A wrongful death action against Trinity and the manufacturer ensued, and Trinity's insurer provided Trinity a defense. A mediation among all parties provided an opportunity to settle the liability against Trinity for less than its $2 million policy limits. The insurer attended the mediation and refused the opportunity to settle. Trinity, fearing a judgment in excess of policy limits, agreed to and paid the settlement.

Trinity then sued its insurer, alleging, *inter alia*, negligent failure to settle and seeking indemnification for the settlement amount. The insurer defended itself by arguing that Trinity had breached the provision in the insurance policy barring insureds from making a "voluntary payment" without the insurer's prior consent. The Supreme Court of Georgia agreed, holding that "an action for negligent or bad faith failure to settle a case requires that a judgment be entered against an insured in excess of the policy limits before the action can be asserted."[107] The court distinguished *Dowse*, in which the insured was "wholly abandon[ed]", reasoning that Trinity's insurer provided a defense and had not breached its duties so as to release Trinity from its duties as an insured. Accordingly, Trinity had no cause of action for bad faith as a matter of law.

§ 3.15 EXPERT WITNESSES IN COMMON-LAW BAD-FAITH ACTIONS

The crux of the typical common-law bad-faith lawsuit turns on the reasonableness of the insurer's decision to decline an opportunity to settle within policy limits.[108] In some cases

---

[107] *Id.* at 583, 10.
[108] *See* § 3.3, *supra*.

expert testimony regarding the insurance company's actions could be helpful for the trier of fact in determining whether the insurer behaved as an "ordinarily prudent insurer" in determining whether to settle a lawsuit.

Although questions as to the appropriateness of a particular expert would be a fact-intensive analysis tailored to a specific case, a few reported cases offer some guidance. Under the familiar *Daubert* standard,[109] the Northern District of Georgia has ruled that an esteemed attorney with 30 years of experience litigating personal injury cases involving automobiles and who has authored an authoritative treatise on the subject was not qualified to provide expert testimony on whether an insurance company properly responded to a time-limited demand to settle within policy limits.[110] The court reasoned that the attorney had never worked in the insurance industry as an adjuster of automobile liability claims. Thus, he was unqualified to testify as to the standard of care for a claims adjuster in receipt of a time-limited demand.[111]

A practicing attorney who is an adjunct professor of insurance law, who had counseled insurers on claims handling and underwriting in a manner "similar to those of a claims manager" and who had authored a treatise on insurance issues was qualified to testify in the Middle District of Georgia.[112] The same expert could not, however, "merely describe what the law is or tell the jury what result to reach."[113]

---

[109]   *Daubert v. Merrell Dow Pharm., Inc.*, 509 U.S. 579 (1993). The same standard now applies in Georgia state court. O.C.G.A. § 24-9-67.1(f).
[110]   *Butler v. First Acceptance Ins. Co., Inc.*, 652 F. Supp. 2d 1264 (N.D. Ga. 2009).
[111]   *Id.* at 1272.
[112]   *Whiteside v. Infinity Cas. Ins. Co.*, 2008 WL 3456508, *7 (M.D. Ga. Aug. 8, 2008).
[113]   *Whiteside v. Infinity Cas. Ins. Co.*, 2008 WL 3456508, *8 (M.D. Ga. Aug. 8, 2008).

An adjuster who had handled thousands of time-limited demand letters in a 30-plus year career with State Farm was unqualified to testify as to industry standards. The court reasoned that the adjuster had worked solely for State Farm during those decades, so he had not shown that he had sufficiently broad knowledge of the industry so as to form opinions regarding industry-wide standards.[114] The court noted that the proffered expert had also been out of the insurance industry for many years, and there was little evidence that the former adjuster had taken steps to keep his knowledge of industry practices current.

Expert testimony on the standard applicable to a "reasonably prudent insurer" is not necessary in all cases.[115] *Dickerson v. Am. Nat'l Property and Ca. Co.* involved the failure of an adjuster to accept a time-limited demand for policy limits. Testimony from the adjuster revealed that the adjuster had no doubt as to the insured's liability or that the claimant's damages exceeded policy limits of $25,000. The court ruled that the lack of expert testimony was not fatal to the plaintiff's bad-faith claim against the insurance company, because a reasonable fact finder could conclude, based on testimony from the insurance company's own employees, that a reasonably prudent insurer would have accepted the time-limited demand.

---

[114] *Butler v. First Acceptance Ins. Co., Inc.*, 652 F. Supp. 2d 1264, 1272-73 (N.D. Ga. 2009).
[115] *Dickerson v. Am. Nat'l Property and Ca. Co.*, 2009 WL 1035131 (M.D. Ga.).

CHAPTER 4

PROCEDURAL ASPECTS OF BAD-FAITH CASES

§ 4.1 PARTIES

As in any litigation, an insured filing suit against its insurer must name the proper party. Litigation involving insurance companies can present challenges in this regard, as many insurers operate myriad companies under similar names. For example, the Georgia Secretary of State website lists no fewer than eight entities beginning with the words "State Farm," six of which would appear to be underwriters of insurance policies. Accordingly, special care must be taken to avoid dismissal for failure to name the proper party.

The declarations page of the insured's policy should state the correct name of the insuring company. Further research is advisable, as insurers frequently merge, are acquired or simply change names. Most insurers maintain detailed websites with information about their companies, and a simple Google search will turn up such information. Information found during such searches should be confirmed by reference to records of the appropriate secretary of state. The Georgia Safety Fire & Insurance Commissioner's website provides a "company search" form.[1] The search form will provide detailed information about the company, including the type of company, the date it was licensed to do business in Georgia, the status of the company's license, the insurer's agents (if any), contact information, and lines of authority (what types of insurance the insurer is licensed to write). In addition, the Georgia Secretary of State's website should reveal current agents for service of process for most companies.[2]

---

[1] Available at http://www.inscomm.state.ga.us/Insurers/CompanySearch.aspx.

[2] Available at http://corp.sos.state.ga.us/corp/soskb/CSearch.asp.

§ 4.2 VENUE

O.C.G.A. § 33-4-1 sets out the venue provisions for actions against insurers.[3] Such actions may be brought:

> (1) in the county where the insurer's principal office is located;
>
> (2) in any county where the insurer has an agent or place of doing business;
>
> (3) in any county where an agent or place of doing business was located when the cause of action accrued;
>
> (4) in any county in which the property covered by the policy is located or where a person entitled to the proceeds of an insurance policy maintains his legal residence.

O.C.G.A. § 33-5-34(a) provides for venue in actions against unauthorized or surplus lines insurers "in the superior court of the county in which the cause of action arose."

§ 4.3 CHOICE OF LAW

Georgia adheres to the traditional rule of *lex loci contractus*.[4] Under the rule, the validity, nature, construction, and interpretation of a contract are governed by the substantive law of the state where the contract was made.[5] In Georgia, an insurance contract is "made" at the place where the contract is delivered.[6] For example, if a Georgia company obtains an insurance policy from a Minnesota insurer and the policy is delivered to the company in Georgia, a Georgia court will

---

[3] O.C.G.A. § 33-4-1 expressly excludes actions against unauthorized insurers or surplus lines contracts. Venue for actions against unauthorized or surplus lines insurers is codified in O.C.G.A. § 33-5-34.

[4] *Convergys Corp. v. Keener*, 276 Ga. 808, 812, 582 S.E.2d 84, 87 (2003).

[5] *Fed. Ins. Co. v. Nat'l Distrib. Co.*, 203 Ga. App. 763, 765, 417 S.E.2d 671, 673 (1992).

[6] *Id.* 203 Ga. App. at 766.

apply Georgia law to the interpretation of the contract. Care should be taken when the insured has corporate officers or uses insurance brokers in places other than Georgia, as the policy may be delivered to a risk manager in an office in Miami or to a broker headquartered in New York.

In 1984, the Georgia Supreme Court expressly rejected the "center of gravity" test outlined in the Restatement (Second) of Conflicts § 188.[7] Nonetheless, litigants should not ignore attempts to apply the concept in the proper case.

Federal courts sitting in diversity apply the forum state's choice-of-law principles.[8] Thus, if the bad-faith case is removed to federal court or initiated by the insurer in federal court, the district court should apply Georgia's rule of *lex loci contractus.*

§ 4.4   SERVICE OF PROCESS

Service of process may be effected differently depending on the type of insurer.

For most "domestic insurers"[9] service of process may be accomplished "in the manner provided by laws applying to corporations generally."[10] Reciprocal insurers[11] and Lloyd's associations[12] may be served in the same manner or upon their attorney in fact.[13]

---

[7] *General Telephone Co. of Southeast v. Trimm,* 252 Ga. 95, 96, 311 S.E.2d 460 (1984).

[8] *Klaxon Co. v. Stentor Elec. Mfg. Co.,* 313 U.S. 487 (1941).

[9] A domestic insurer is an insurer incorporated or formed under the laws of the State of Georgia. *Aetna Cas. & Sur. Co. v. Sampley,* 108 Ga. App. 617, 621, 134 S.E.2d 71 (1963).

[10] O.C.G.A. § 33-4-2.

[11] A system of insurance where several individuals or agents act through an agent to underwrite one another's risks, making each insured an insurer of the other members of the group. *Black's Law Dictionary* (1996).

[12] A voluntary association of merchants, shipowners, underwriters and brokers that does not write policies but that issues a notice of an endeavor to members who may individually underwrite a policy by assuming shares of the

Alien[14] or foreign[15] insurers must file with the Georgia Insurance Commissioner a power of attorney appointing a resident of Georgia to receive service of process.[16] The power of attorney is irrevocable and may only be terminated by the filing of a new appointment by the insurer.[17] Alien or foreign insurers must also appoint the Georgia Insurance Commissioner as its attorney to receive service of process.[18] A party attempting to serve an alien or foreign insurer can only serve the Commissioner if service upon the attorney-in-fact cannot be effected.[19]

Service upon nonresident religious or mutual aid societies and certain other cooperative insurers may be made by personal service upon certain officers or certain officers of local lodges.[20]

Unauthorized or surplus lines insurers are deemed to have appointed the Georgia Insurance Commissioner as their attorney for acceptance of service of process issued in Georgia for any action or proceeding arising out of the policy.[21] Surplus lines policies must contain a provision stating the substance of O.C.G.A. § 33-5-34(b) and designating a person to whom the Commissioner will mail process according to O.C.G.A. § 33-5-34(d).[22]

---

total risk of insuring a client; the names of the bound underwriters and the attorney-in-fact appear on the policy. *Blacks Law Dictionary* (1996).

[13]   O.C.G.A. § 33-4-2.

[14]   An insurance company incorporated or formed under the laws of a country other than the United States. *Aetna Cas. & Sur. Co. v. Sampley*, 108 Ga. App. 617, 621, 134 S.E.2d 71 (1963).

[15]   An insurance company incorporated or formed under the laws of another State or government of the United States. *Id.* 108 Ga. App. at 621.

[16]   O.C.G.A. § 33-4-3(1).

[17]   *Id.*

[18]   O.C.G.A. § 33-4-3(2)

[19]   *Id.*

[20]   O.C.G.A. § 33-4-5

[21]   O.C.G.A. § 33-5-34(b)

[22]   O.C.G.A. § 33-5-34(c)

§ 4.5   DECLARATORY JUDGMENTS

Many lawsuits involving insurance coverage or an insurer's bad faith unfold in the context of a declaratory judgment.[23] This section addresses those issues specific to a declaratory judgment action involving insurers and insureds. The Georgia Declaratory Judgment Act, O.C.G.A. § 9-4-1 *et seq.* provides a mechanism to settle and afford relief from uncertainty and insecurity with respect to rights, status, and other legal relations.[24]

In Georgia, "a declaratory judgment is permitted to determine a controversy before obligations are repudiated or rights are violated."[25] The petitioner is not entitled to a declaratory judgment where the rights of the parties have already accrued and there are no circumstances showing any necessity for a determination of the dispute to guide and protect the petitioner from uncertainty and insecurity with regard to the propriety of some future act or conduct.[26] A declaratory judgment action makes no provision for a judgment which is advisory.[27]

With respect to disputes involving insurance coverage, the Supreme Court of Georgia provided four factors to be considered in determining whether a declaratory judgment is proper under a given set of facts:

---

[23]   The Georgia Declaratory Judgment Act, O.C.G.A. § 9-4-1 *et seq.*, applies in state court only. The federal version, 28 U.S.C.A. § 2201, applies in federal district court. Care should be taken, as the federal act is interpreted more broadly than the Georgia version with respect to declaratory judgment actions initiated by insurers who have denied coverage.

[24]   O.C.G.A. § 9-4-1.

[25]   *Colonial Ins. Co. of Calif. v. Progressive Casualty Ins. Co.*, 252 Ga. App. 391, 392, 556 S.E.2d (2001).

[26]   *Morgan v. Guaranty National Companies*, 268 Ga. 343, 344, 489 S.E.2d 803 (1997), citing *State Farm Mut. Auto. Ins. Co. v. Hillhouse*, 131 Ga.App. 524, 525, 206 S.E.2d 627 (1974).

[27]   *Id., citing Hillhouse*, 131 Ga.App. at 525-526.

(1) a demand for payment has been made;
(2) the insurance company has not yet acted to deny the claim;
(3) legitimate questions exist about the validity and applicability of the policy clause; and
(4) Georgia law does not provide a clear answer.[28]

Where circumstances cast doubt on whether a liability policy provides coverage for a claim, there is such an immediacy of choice imposed upon an insurer that an insurer is entitled to seek a declaratory judgment.[29] If an insurer is uncertain how to handle a claim made on a policy, the insurer may enter a defense for the insured under a reservation of rights and then seek a declaratory judgment.[30] For example, if a liability insurer indicates there will be no coverage for a particular claim prior to suit being filed against the insured, and the insurer assumes the defense once the lawsuit is filed, the insurer may pursue a declaratory judgment.[31]

However, an insurer may *not* file a declaratory judgment action after judgment has been taken against the insured, because there is no uncertainty and insecurity as to future conduct between the parties.[32] A declaratory judgment is

---

[28] *Adams v. Atlanta Cas. Co.*, 225 Ga. App. 482, 485, 484 S.E.2d 302 (1997).

[29] *Richmond v. Georgia Farm Bureau Mut. Ins. Co.*, 140 Ga. App. 215, 217, 231 S.E.2d 245 (1976), citing *Nationwide Mut. Ins. Co. v. Peek*, 112 Ga. App. 260, 263, 145 S.E.2d 50 (1965).

[30] *Morgan v. Guaranty National Companies*, 268 Ga. 343, 344, 489 S.E.2d 803 (1997), citing *Bowen v. Georgia Farm Bureau Mut. Ins. Co.*, 162 Ga. App. 707, 708, 293 S.E.2d 8 (1982). *See also Richmond v. Georgia Farm Bureau Mut. Ins. Co.*, 140 Ga.App. 215, 217, 231 S.E.2d 245 (1976) ("A proper and safe course of action for an insurer in this position is to enter upon a defense under a reservation of rights and then proceed to seek a declaratory judgment in its favor.").

[31] *Danforth v. Government Employees Ins. Co.*, 282 Ga. App. 421, 424, 638 S.E.2d 852 (2006), citing *Colonial Ins. Co. of Calif. v. Progressive Casualty Ins. Co.*, 252 Ga. App. 391, 392-393, 556 S.E.2d 486 (2001).

[32] *Thomas v. Atlanta Cas. Co.*, 253 Ga. App. 199, 200, 558 S.E.2d 432 (2001), citing *Empire Fire & Marine Ins. Co. v. Metro Courier Corp.*, 234 Ga. App.

also not available merely to test the viability of a party's defenses.[33] An insurer may not refuse to pay under its policy
and then use the declaratory judgment procedure to avoid
bad-faith penalties.[34] To allow an insurance company to file
a declaratory judgment when it has already taken a defini-
tive position as to coverage would frustrate the purpose of
the Declaratory Judgment Act.[35] Even where the insurer did
not expressly determine prior to the entry of the judgment
that the policy did not provide coverage for the insured, the
failure to provide a defense to the insured is equivalent to a
denial of coverage and prevents an insurer from later seeking a declaratory judgment.[36]

In *Drawdy v. Direct General Ins. Co.*,[37] the Supreme Court of
Georgia held that an insurer was precluded from bringing a
declaratory judgment action after an unqualified denial of
coverage to the insured. The claims in this case arose from a
fatal auto accident caused by the insured's nephew who was
driving the insured's vehicle. A month after the accident,
the insurer unconditionally denied coverage because its investigation revealed that the insured's nephew was driving
the vehicle without the insured's knowledge or permission.[38]
Later, the insurer filed a declaratory judgment action. No
tort action had been filed against the insured or his nephew
at that point and the insurer expressly stated in its complaint that it had denied coverage. The insured moved to

---

670, 671-672, 507 S.E.2d 525 (1998); *Hatcher v. Georgia Farm Bureau Mut. Ins. Co.*, 112 Ga. App. 711, 716-717, 146 S.E.2d 535 (1965).

[33] *Morgan v. Guaranty National Companies*, 268 Ga. 343, 345, 489 S.E.2d 803 (1997), citing *Sentry Ins. v. Majeed*, 194 Ga.App. 276, 276, 390 S.E.2d 269 (1990), *aff'd* 260 Ga. 203, 391 S.E.2d 649 (1990).

[34] *Morgan v. Guaranty National Companies*, 268 Ga. 343, 344, 489 S.E.2d 803 (1997), citing *State Farm Mut. Auto. Ins. Co. v. Allstate Ins. Co.*, 132 Ga. App. 332, 334, 208 S.E.2d 170 (1974).

[35] *Atlanta Cas. Co. v. Fountain*, 262 Ga. 16, 18, 413 S.E.2d 450 (1992).

[36] *Morgan v. Guaranty National Companies*, 268 Ga. 343, 344, 489 S.E.2d 803 (1997).

[37] *Drawdy v. Direct General Ins. Co.*, 277 Ga. 107, 586 S.E.2d 228 (2003).

[38] *Id.* 277 Ga. at 108.

dismiss the declaratory judgment.[39] One week after the motion to dismiss was filed, the estate of the passenger in the car filed suit against the insured. The insurer apparently defended the suit under a reservation of rights.[40] In reversing the Court of Appeals, the Supreme Court stated that a declaratory judgment was not authorized in this case because Direct General had denied the claim and was not uncertain or insecure in regard to its rights, status, or legal relations. The Supreme Court distinguished *Colonial Ins. Co. of Calif. v. Progressive Casualty Ins. Co.*, noting that in that case the insurer had sent a "qualified denial" and undertook the insured's defense under a reservation of rights *before* filing a declaratory judgment action.[41] Finally, the Supreme Court noted that the purpose of the Declaratory Judgment Act is to protect parties from uncertainty as to *future* conduct, not from the adverse consequences of actions already taken.[42]

Provided that coverage has not been denied, an insurer may file a post-judgment declaratory judgment action to determine whether the policy provides coverage to the insured. The insured may pursue action for breach of contract.[43] An insured has the same right to seek a declaratory judgment as the insurer.[44] Allowing insureds to file declaratory judgment actions "levels the playing field" between insurers and insureds.[45]

When an insurer or insured files a declaratory judgment action seeking guidance on whether the insurer must defend an "underlying lawsuit" against the insured, the question

---

[39] *Id*. 277 Ga. at 108.
[40] *Id*. 277 Ga. at 108.
[41] *Id*. 277 Ga. at 109 (emphasis in original).
[42] *Id*. 277 Ga. at 109 (citations omitted and emphasis added).
[43] *Atlanta Cas. Co. v. Fountain*, 262 Ga. 16, 413 S.E.2d 450 (1992).
[44] *Atlantic Wood Industries, Inc. v. Argonaut Ins. Co.*, 258 Ga. 800, 375 S.E.2d 221 (1989), *rev'g* 187 Ga.App. 471, 370 S.E.2d 765 (1988).
[45] *Id*. 258 Ga. at 801.

sometimes arises whether the underlying lawsuit or the declaratory judgment should be first decided. Whether a stay of the underlying lawsuit will be granted is in the discretion of the court.

CHAPTER 5

SPECIAL ISSUES IN INSURANCE LITIGATION

§ 5.1   INTRODUCTION

All litigation regarding an insurer's bad faith necessarily involves other issues associated with the law of insurance contracts and insurance coverage. For example, an insurer's bad-faith failure to settle under the common law may have its genesis in the insurance company's decision not to provide a defense to an insured, the lack of defense resulting in a large judgment in excess of policy limits. With respect to statutory bad faith, issues may arise as to whether the insurer's decision not to pay a property damage claim is caused by the insurer's failure to conduct an adequate investigation. Finally, any time there is litigation involving any type of insurance policy, certain issues – like timely notice – might come into play. Though this treatise is not intended to comprehensively cover all such issues, several of those most common to bad-faith litigation are discussed below.

§ 5.2   DUTY TO GIVE NOTICE / LIABILITY POLICIES

An insured's failure to provide notice of a claim or of a lawsuit to its liability carrier can defeat coverage. The standard commercial general liability policy provides that "[i]f a claim is made or suit is brought against any insured," the insured must notify the insurer "as soon as practicable."[1] Other policies might provide for "immediate" notice upon knowledge of a suit or claim. The Georgia Legislature has decreed that automobile liability policies shall require notice of a suit as well as delivery to the insurer of a copy of the summons and process.[2] As suggested below, and as made more clear by a reading of the cases, different language in an insurance pol-

---

[1]   ISO CG 00 01 10 01, © ISO Properties, Inc., 2000.
[2]   O.C.G.A. § 33-7-15.

icy's notice provision can lead to different results. Accordingly, despite what courts before have decided, the insured's duty of notice must be analyzed in relation to the specific policy language and the applicable facts.

The purpose of notice is to inform the insurer of potential liability so that it may promptly investigate the circumstances, prepare a defense, or consider the prudence of payment, settlement or other resolution.[3] Under certain circumstances, therefore, delay may prejudice the insurer's ability to control the defense of the case.[4] If notice is a condition precedent to coverage under the policy, however, an insurer does not need to demonstrate that late notice caused prejudice in order to deny coverage.[5] The lack of prejudice can, however, be a factor for consideration in determining whether notice is untimely under the circumstances.[6] Also, "an insured is not required to foresee every possible claim, no matter how remote, that might arise from an event and give notice of it to his insurer. Instead, the law only requires an insured to act reasonably under the circumstances."[7]

---

[3] *Southeastern Exp. Systems, Inc. v. Southern Guaranty Ins. Co. of Georgia*, 224 Ga. App. 697, 701 482 S.E.2d 433 (1997), citing *Public Nat. Ins. Co. v. Wheat*, 1 Ga. App. 695, 698, 112 S.E.2d 194 (1959) and *Kitt v. Shield Ins. Co.*, 840 Ga. 619, 621, 241 S.E.2d 824 (1978). *See also Richmond v. Georgia Farm Bureau Mut. Ins. Co.*, 140 Ga. App. 215, 221, 231 S.E.2d 245 (1976) ("The purpose of the notice provision in an insurance policy is to enable an insurer to investigate promptly the facts surrounding the occurrence while they are still fresh and the witnesses are still available, to prepare for a defense of the action, and, in a proper case, to determine the feasibility of settlement of the claim.").

[4] *Southeastern Exp. Systems, Inc. v. Southern Guaranty Ins. Co. of Georgia*, 224 Ga. App. 697, 701 482 S.E.2d 433 (1997).

[5] *Caldwell v. State Farm Fire & Cas. Ins. Co.*, 192 Ga. App. 419, 420, 385 S.E.2d 97 (1989), citing *Richmond v. Georgia Farm Bureau Mut. Ins. Co.*, 140 Ga. App. 215, 222, 231 S.E.2d 245 (1976) (an insurer is not required to show that it was prejudiced by the failure to give notice where the requirement is a valid condition precedent to coverage).

[6] *See, OneBeacon Am. Ins. Co. v. Catholic Diocese of Savannah*, 477 F. App'x 665, 672 (11th Cir. 2012) (citing to Georgia cases).

[7] *Forshee v. Employers Mut. Cas. Co.*, 309 Ga. App. 621, 623, 711 S.E.2d 28, 31 (2011), *cert. denied* (Oct. 3, 2011).

Where an insured has not demonstrated justification for failure to give notice according to the terms of the policy, and where the insurer has not waived compliance, the insurer is not obligated to provide a defense and coverage is void.[8] In most cases involving an automobile liability policy, on the other hand, Georgia law requires the insurer to prove that late notice caused prejudice.[9]

Although most policies require notice from the actual insured, a third party, including an attorney for the injured party, can give notice to the insurer of the action in order to prevent the insurer from raising a late-notice defense.[10] "It makes no difference who gives the notice, so long as a reasonable and timely notice is given the company and it has actual knowledge of the pendency of a claim or suit."[11] In *Hathaway Dev. Co., Inc. v. Am. Empire Surplus Lines Ins. Co.*, the liability insurer received notice of the lawsuit from the claimant in accordance with O.C.G.A. § 33-7-15(a). Although the court noted that the statute applied only to automobile liability policies, the court nonetheless relied on older cases to rule that "[n]otice from [the claimant] was sufficient under [the insured's] CGL policy to fulfill the contractual condition of notice."[12]

Notice to an insurance broker may not suffice as notice to the insurance company if the broker is an independent agent (or an agent of the insured) and the policy's notice provision

---

[8]   *Richmond v. Georgia Farm Bureau Mut. Ins. Co.*, 140 Ga. App. 215, 221, 231 S.E.2d 245 (1976) (citing numerous cases).

[9]   O.C.G.A. § 33-7-15(b).

[10]   *Atlanta Casualty Company v. Thomas*, 253 Ga. App. 199, 203, 558 S.E.2d (2001) (*citing* O.C.G.A. § 33-7-15(a)).

[11]   *Hathaway Dev. Co., Inc. v. Am. Empire Surplus Lines Ins. Co.*, 301 Ga. App. 65, 68, 686 S.E.2d 855, 860 (2009), *aff'd*, 288 Ga. 749, 707 S.E.2d 369 (2011).

[12]   301 Ga. App. at 68, 686 S.E.2d at 860 (*citing Stonewall Ins. Co. v. Farone*, 129 Ga.App. 471, 474, 199 S.E.2d 852 (1973) (timely forwarding of suit by injured plaintiff to tortfeasor's insurer sufficient to invoke coverage under policy); *Rowe v. Ga. Cas. etc. Co.*, 158 Ga.App. 159, 165(3), 279 S.E.2d 318 (1981).

does not extend such apparent authority to the independent agent.[13]

Georgia courts generally construe the policy requirements that notice be "prompt" or "as soon as practicable"[14] as requiring that notice be given in a reasonable time under the circumstances.[15] An insured cannot always wait to provide notice until after the repercussions of an accident become fully known and fully appreciated. Instead, it is the nature and the circumstances of "the incident and the immediate conclusions an ordinarily prudent and reasonable person would draw there from that determine whether an insured has reasonably justified his decision not to notify the insurer."[16] Whether an insured gives notice under a policy "promptly" or "as soon as practicable" is generally a question of fact for the jury[17] and not an issue for summary judgment.[18] If the undisputed facts and circumstances indicate

---

[13] *Southeastern Exp. Systems, Inc. v. Southern Guar. Ins. Co. of Georgia*, 224 Ga. App. 697, 700, 482 S.E.2d 433 (1997).

[14] "Prompt" and "as soon as practicable" are synonymous terms. *See Haston v. Transamerica Ins. Services*, 662 So.2d 1138, 1141 (Ala. 1995) ("the term 'prompt' notice, as used in the contract of insurance ... is synonymous with notice terms such as 'immediately' and 'as soon as practicable,' which have been held to mean that 'notice must be given within a reasonable time in view of the facts and circumstances of the case.' ").

[15] Couch on Insurance § 190:31 (2008); *Brown v. State Farm Mut. Auto Cas. Ins. Co.*, 506 F.2d 976, 978 (5th Cir. 1975) ("A requirement in a policy of prompt or immediate notice generally means that the notice must be given within a reasonable time in view of all of the facts and circumstances of the case.").

[16] *Southern Gar. Ins. Co. v. Miller*, 183 Ga. App. 261, 263, 358 S.E.2d 611 (1987).

[17] *United Services Automobile Association v. Middleton*, 77 F.R.D. 660 (N.D. Ga. 1978), citing *State Farm Mutual Automobile Ins. Co. v. Coleman*, 441 F.2d 329 (5th Cir. 1971); *State Farm Mutual Automobile Ins. Co. v. Sloan*, 150 Ga. App. 464, 466, 258 S.E.2d 146 (1979); *Plantation Pipeline Co. v. Royal Indem. Co.*, 245 Ga. App. 23, 25, 537 S.E.2d 165 (2000); *Weis v. International Insurance Company, Inc.*, 567 F. Supp. 631, 635 (N.D. Ga. 1983) (citing numerous cases).

[18] *United States Automobile Association v. Middleton*, 77 F.R.D. 660, 661-662 (N.D. Ga. 1978), citing *State Farm Mutual Automobile Ins. Co. v. Coleman*, 441 F.2d 329, 331 (5th Cir. 1971) (Whether an insured reported an accident "as soon as practicable" "depends on the facts and circumstances of the case, measured by an objective standard from the viewpoint of the policyholder ... As such it is not an appropriate issue for summary judgment."); *State Farm Mutual*

that an insured's delay in giving notice was unjustified and unreasonable, the court may rule on the question as a matter of law."[19] Under the facts and circumstances of the following cases, notice was late as a matter of law:

8 months - *Southeastern Exp. Systems, Inc.v. Southern Guaranty Ins. Co. of Georgia*, 224 Ga.App. 697, 482 S.E.2d 433 (1997); *Richmond v. Georgia Farm Bureau Mut. Ins. Co.*, 140 Ga.App. 215, 216, 231 S.E.2d 245 (1976).

13 months - *Briggs & Stratton Corp. v. Royal Globe Ins. Co.*, 64 F.Supp.2d 1346 (1999).

22 months – *Aegis Security Ins. Co. v. Hiers*, 211 Ga.App. 639, 440 S.E.2d 71 (1994).

38 months – *Brazil v. Government Employees Ins. Co.*, 199 Ga.App 343, 404 S.E.2d 807 (1991).

52 months – *International Indem. Co. v. Smith*, 178 Ga.App. 4. 342 S.E.2d 4 (1986).

Automobile Ins. Co. v. Sloan, 150 Ga. App. 464, 466, 258 S.E.2d 146 (1979) ("[Q]uestions [about] the adequacy of the notice and the merit of [claims] of justification are ones of fact which must be resolved by a jury as they are not susceptible to being summarily adjudicated as a matter of law."); *Plantation Pipeline Co. v. Royal Indem. Co.*, 245 Ga. App. 23, 25, 537 S.E.2d 165 (2000) (It is the province of the jury to determine whether an excuse or justification was sufficient and whether the insured acted diligently in giving notice "according to the nature and circumstances of each individual case."); *Weis v. International Ins. Co.*, 567 F. Supp. 631, 635 (N.D. Ga. 1983) (citing numerous cases) ("A long line of cases interpreting policy provisions that require notice of loss to the insurer 'as soon as practicable'... have uniformly held that whether notice is timely is a question for the jury to determine in light of all of the circumstances of the case.").

[19] *Caldwell v. State Farm Fire & Cas. Ins. Co.*, 192 Ga. App. 419, 420-421, 385 S.E.2d 97 (1989), citing *Richmond v. Georgia Farm Bureau Ins. Co.*, 140 Ga. App. 215, 220-221, 231 S.E.2d 245 (1976). *See also Townsend v. National Fire Ins. Co.*, 196 Ga. App. 789, 789, 397 S.E.2d 61 (1990) ("whether or not the condition [of notice] has been met is not always a jury question because an unexcused significant delay may be unreasonable as a matter of law.").

70 months – *Townsend v. Nat'l Union Fire Co.*, 196 Ga.App. 789, 397 S.E.2d 61 (1990).

5 years - *South Carolina Ins. Co. v. Moody*, 957 F.Supp. 234 (M.D. Ga. 1997).

25 years - *Plantation Pipeline Co. v. Royal Indem. Co.*, 245 Ga.App. 23, 537 S.E.2d 165 (2000).

However, lapse of time alone is not sufficient to establish non-compliance with the notice provision.[20] "In most cases, however, the reasonableness of a failure to give notice is a question for the finder of fact."[21] "Whether reasonableness can be decided as a matter of law, or whether it should remain in the province of the jury depends on two factors: the sufficiency of the excuse, and the insured's diligence after any disability has been removed."[22] *OneBeacon Am. Ins. Co. v. Catholic Diocese of Savannah* involved a delay in notice 21 months after the insured was served with the lawsuit. The insured argued that the delay was justified because the claim triggered policies that were many years old and that could not be quickly located. The insured submitted an affidavit from its counsel attesting to the justification. The Eleventh Circuit affirmed a ruling that the delay was unreasonable as a matter of law. Although the court recognized that a 21-month is not always unreasonable as a matter of law, the affidavit was conclusory, bereft of critical dates and failed to raise a fact issue as how the delay was excused or justified.[23]

---

[20] *JNJ Foundation Specialists, Inc. v. D.R. Horton, Inc.*, 311 Ga.App. 269, 275, 717 S.E.2d 219 (2011).
[21] *Forshee v. Employers Mut. Cas. Co.*, 309 Ga. App. 621, 624, 711 S.E.2d 28, 31 (2011), *cert. denied*, (Oct. 3, 2011).
[22] *See, OneBeacon Am. Ins. Co. v. Catholic Diocese of Savannah*, 477 F. App'x 665, 671 (11th Cir. 2012) (citing to Georgia cases).
[23] 477 F. App'x at 671.

Where the insured has no knowledge of a claim, courts have generally found that the issue of whether notice is timely is for the jury. For example, in *United Services Automobile Association v. Middleton*,[24] the defendant was involved in an accident with another car. At the time of the accident, there were no visible injuries, and the driver and passengers stated that they were not injured. The first notice of injuries came in a letter from the other driver's attorney nine months after the loss, at which time the insured reported the loss. The court denied the insurer's motion for summary judgment.[25] Similarly, in *Norfolk & Dedham Mut. Fire Ins. Co. v. Cumbaa*,[26] the Court of Appeals held that a jury issue existed as to whether a 19-month delay in providing notice was timely because substantial evidence of the claim did not come to the insured until that time.

Justification for failure to give notice as soon as practicable may not include the insured's unfounded conclusion that there was no liability to the other party. It is the insurer's job to reasonably investigate the issues of liability and damages.[27] An insured is not required, however, to foresee every possible claim that could arise from an incident.[28] In *Newberry v. Cotton States Mut. Ins. Co.*, the insured attended a work-related social function and fought with another guest.[29] The insured did not notify its insurer until 14 days after being served with a complaint. The insured testified that he believed any claims arising from the incident would be han-

---

[24] *United States Automobile Association v. Middleton*, 77 F.R.D. 660 (N.D. Ga. 1978).

[25] *Id.* 77 F.R.D. at 661.

[26] *Norfolk & Dedham Mut. Fire Ins. Co. v. Cumbaa*, 128 Ga. App. 196, 198, 196 S.E.2d 167 (1973).

[27] *Richmond v. Georgia Farm Bureau Mut. Ins. Co.*, 140 Ga. App. 215, 220, 231 S.E.2d 245 (1976), citing *Bituminous Cas. Corp. v. J.B. Forrest & Sons, Inc.*, 132 Ga. App. 714, 717, 20 S.E.2d 6 (1974).

[28] *Newberry v. Cotton States Mut. Ins. Co.*, 242 Ga. App. 784, 785, 531 S.E.2d 362 (2000).

[29] *Id.*

dled through worker's compensation.[30] The Court of Appeals held that an insured is not required to foresee every possible claim but is required only to act reasonably under the circumstances, creating an issue for the jury's determination.[31]

In *Forshee v. Employers Mut. Cas. Co.*[32], the Court of Appeals explained:

> Sometimes an event is so trivial or inconsequential that a court properly may conclude as a matter of law that no reasonable person would think that a claim could arise from the event and, therefore, that no notice of the event is required...it is the nature and circumstances of the accident or the incident and the immediate conclusions an ordinarily prudent and reasonable person would draw therefrom that determine whether an insured has reasonably justified his decision not to notify the insurer. Relevant circumstances include the nature of the event, the extent to which it would appear to a reasonable person in the circumstances of the insured that injuries or property damage resulted from the event, and the apparent severity of any such injuries or damages...A court also properly may consider whether anyone gave an indication that he intended to hold the insured responsible for the event and resulting injuries and the extent to which the insured acknowledged the likelihood that a claim could arise from the event, either by offering compensation to the injured person or asking him to sign a release...And a trial court must make every effort to eliminate the

---

[30]   *Id.*
[31]   *Id.*
[32]   309 Ga.App. 621, 711 S.E.2d 28 (2011), *cert. denied*, (Oct. 3, 2011).

distorting effects of hindsight and to evaluate
the conduct of the insured from the perspective
of a reasonable person in the same circumstances as those in which the insured found
himself.[33]

In cases where the policy requires notice "as soon as practicable," an insured's failure to give notice due to a lack of
knowledge that coverage existed may be a jury question. In
Georgia Mutual Ins. Co. v. Criterion Ins. Co.,[34] the insureds
failed to give notice to the insurer for four months because
they did not know their policy provided coverage for a new
car. The Court of Appeals held that the issue of late notice
was a jury issue. In *State Farm Mut. Automobile Ins. Co. v.
Sloan*,[35] the insureds believed there would be no insurance
coverage for an accident and did not give notice to their insurer for six months because their son was driving the car,
the son was not named as an insured, and the son was driving a car not covered by the insurance policy. Again, the
Court of Appeals held that whether the insureds notified
their insurance company "as soon as practicable" was an issue to be determined by a jury.

In contrast, where a policy provides that notice be given
"immediately," failure to give notice may be subject to determination as a matter of law. In *Hill v. Safeco Insurance
Company of America*,[36] the Middle District of Georgia
granted the insurer's motion for summary judgment as to
the insured's failure to comply with the notice provision of
his policy. The insured was required to give "immediate notice" to Safeco of the loss. The insured failed to give notice

---

[33] *Id.* at 624 (citations omitted).
[34] *Georgia Mut. Ins. Co. v. Criterion Ins. Co.*, 131 Ga. App. 339, 206
S.E.2d 88 (1974).
[35] *State Farm Mut. Auto. Ins. Co. v. Sloan*,150 Ga. App. 464, 258 S.E.2d
146 (1979).
[36] *Hill v. Safeco Ins. Co. of America*, 93 F. Supp. 2d 1375 (M.D. Ga. 1999).

for six months because he did not believe his policy provided coverage for the loss.

If an insured fails to give notice of a complaint and summons as required by a policy and later provides notice of an amended complaint, each notice is subject to separate analysis.[37] In other words, there is no "blanket rule" that if notice of an initial complaint is untimely, notice of an amended complaint is not necessarily untimely if it alleges new claims.[38]

§ 5.3 DUTY TO GIVE NOTICE / UM COVERAGE

"UM" coverage is an optional coverage that an insured may purchase to cover the insured who is injured by the negligence of another person who has no liability coverage or insufficient liability coverage to compensate the insured for his or her injuries.[39] Like any insurance policy, an automobile policy providing UM coverage will have its own provisions regarding notice of a claim to the insurer.[40] Care must be taken in reading the policy to determine whether the General Conditions section of the policy contains a notice provision applicable to all coverages or whether the UM coverage section contains its own notice provision.[41]

Some general notice provisions that require notice to the insurer within a specified time period have been construed to begin to run following the date of the accident and not the

---

[37] *State Farm Fire & Cas. Co. v. LeBlanc*, 2012 WL 5199253, *6 (11th Cir. Oct. 22, 2012).

[38] *Id.*

[39] *See generally*, O.C.G.A. § 33-7-11.

[40] The timing of service of process on a UM carrier is a separate issue and is addressed by O.C.G.A. § 33-7-11(d) (requiring service of process on a UM carrier at beginning of lawsuit if "a reasonable belief exists that the vehicle is an uninsured motor vehicle" or, "[i]f facts arise after an action has been commenced which create a reasonable belief that a vehicle is an uninsured motor vehicle" 90 days after the party seeking relief discovers or should have discovered the underinsured status).

[41] *See*, Reading an Insurance Policy, §1.11, *supra*.

date the insured learns that the tortfeasor may be uninsured or underinsured.[42] In *Manzi v. Cotton States Mut. Ins. Co.,* the insured was injured in an auto accident. More than six months after the accident she learned that the tortfeasor who had injured her was underinsured, so she provided notice to her insurer that she would seek proceeds from her UM coverage. The policy contained a general notice provision requiring that the insurer be "notified promptly, but in no event later than 60 days, of how when and where the accident or loss happened."[43] The policy did not specifically mention when the 60-day period began to run or what event triggered the notice requirement. The Court of Appeals ruled that the provision was not ambiguously silent, as the surrounding policy language made it clear that the 60-day period began to run at the time of the accident. The court concluded that the insured had breached the notice provision as a matter of law. Because the provision further stated that it "shall be a condition precedent to the existence of any coverage," the insured was unable to recover her UM benefits.[44] A different outcome results, and fact issues are raised with regard to timely notice, when the provision requires notice "as soon as practicable."[45]

In the event that the uninsured or underinsured driver is unknown, the insured "shall immediately" report the accident to law enforcement.[46] The requirement is a condition

---

[42] *Manzi v. Cotton States Mut. Ins. Co.,* 243 Ga. App. 277, 531 S.E.2d 164 (2000).

[43] 243 Ga. App. at 277, 531 S.E.2d at 165.

[44] 243 Ga. App. at 277, 531 S.E.2d at 165.

[45] *Gregory v. Allstate Ins. Co.,* 134 Ga. App. 461, 214 S.E.2d 696 (1975).

[46] O.C.G.A. § 33-7-11(c) (referring to O.C.G.A. § 40-6-273, which requires that "[t]he driver of a vehicle involved in an accident resulting in injury to or death of any person or property damage to an apparent extent of $500.00 or more shall immediately, by the quickest means of communication, give notice of such accident to [law enforcement of the jurisdiction]").

precedent to recovery of UM benefits, and a delay of only "four or five days" following the accident bars UM coverage.[47]

§ 5.4   DUTY TO DEFEND

An important value provided by a liability policy is the insurer's promise to retain attorneys to handle the defense of a lawsuit on behalf of an insured. An insurer's failure to defend sometimes accompanies the insurer's failure to take advantage of a reasonable opportunity to settle within policy limits, making the failure to defend relevant to bad faith. A typical commercial general liability policy includes the following:

> We will pay those sums that the insured becomes legally obligated to pay as damages because of "bodily injury" or "property damage" to which this insurance applies. We will have the right and duty to defend the insured against any "suit" seeking those damages. However, we will have no duty to defend the insured against any "suit" seeking damages for "bodily injury" or "property damage" to which this insurance does not apply. We may, at our discretion, investigate any "occurrence" and settle any claim or "suit" that may result.[48]

An insurer's duty to defend turns on the language of the insurance contract and the allegations of the complaint asserted against the insured.[49] The duty to defend is broad, and "it is only where the complaint sets forth true factual allegations showing no coverage that the suit is one for which liability insurance coverage is not afforded and for

---

[47]   *Navarro v. Atlanta Cas. Co.*, 250 Ga. App. 550, 552 S.E.2d 508 (2001), and *Pender v. Doe*, 276 Ga. App. 178, 622 S.E.2d 888 (2005).

[48]   CG 00 01 10 01, © ISO Properties, Inc., 2000.

[49]   *City of Atlanta v. St. Paul Fire & Marine Ins. Co.*, 231 Ga. App. 206, 207, 498 S.E.2d 782 (1998), citing *Canal Indem. Co. v. Chastain*, 228 Ga. App. 255, 256, 491 S.E.2d 474 (1997) and *Great Am. Ins. Co. v. McKemie*, 244 Ga. 84, 85-86, 259 S.E.2d 39 (1979).

Special Issues in Insurance Litigation 111

which the insurer need not provide a defense."[50] The insurer
is obligated to defend where the allegations of the complaint
against the insured are ambiguous or incomplete with respect to the issue of insurance coverage.[51] The duty to defend is triggered if the complaint shows only "potential" or
"arguable" coverage.[52] The insurer must liberally construe
coverage and defend even if there is only a possibility of coverage.[53] Any doubt as to liability and the insurer's duty to
defend should be resolved in favor of the insured.[54] A carrier
is relieved of the duty to defend only if it is clear that the
plaintiff can prove no set of facts entitling him to relief.[55]
When a plaintiff alleges alternative theories of liability,
there is a duty to defend even if a single alternative impli-
cates coverage.[56] The Georgia Court of Appeals has restated
these rules as follows:

> [A]n insurer is obligated to defend even where the al-
> legations of the complaint against the insured are
> ambiguous or incomplete with respect to the issue of
> insurance coverage. To excuse the duty to defend, the
> petition must unambiguously exclude coverage under
> the policy, and thus, the duty to defend exists if the
> claim potentially comes within the policy. Where the
> claim is one of potential coverage, doubt as to liability

---

[50] *Penn-America Ins. Co. v. Disabled Am. Veterans, Inc.*, 268 Ga. 564,
566, 490 S.E.2d 374 (1997) (affirming trial court's grant of summary judgment in
favor of insureds).

[51] *Id.*

[52] *Id. See also City of Atlanta v. St. Paul Fire & Marine Ins. Co.*, 231 Ga.
App. 206, 207, 498 S.E.2d (1998) ("If the facts as alleged in the complaint even
arguably bring the occurrence within the policy's coverage, the insurer has a duty
to defend the action.").

[53] *Colonial Oil Indust., Inc. v. Underwriters Subscribing to Policy Nos.
TO31504670 and TO31504671*, 268 Ga. 561, 562, 491 S.E.2d 337 (1997).

[54] *Elan Pharm. Research Corp. v. Employers Ins. of Wausau*, 144 F.3d
1372, 1375 (11th Cir. 1998).

[55] *See, e.g., Anderson v. Southern Guar. Ins. Co. of Ga.*, 235 Ga. App. 306,
308-309, 508 S.E.2d 726 (1998).

[56] *Utica Mut. Ins. Co. v. Kelly & Cohen*, 233 Ga. App. 555, 556, 504
S.E.2d 510 (1998), *cert. denied*, Dec. 4, 1998.

and insurer's duty to defend should be resolved in favor of the insured.[57]

A recent example of the application of these rules is *Landmark Am. Ins. Co. v. Khan*.[58] In that case, a claimant was shot while leaving a nightclub. The claimant filed a premises liability lawsuit against the insured nightclub, alleging, *inter alia*, assault and battery by employees of the club. The insurer denied coverage and refused to defend, relying on an assault and battery exclusion in the policy. The exclusion had an exception stating that it did not apply if the assault and battery was committed by an employee of the insured while reasonably protecting persons or property.[59] A default judgment in the amount of $2.3 million was entered against the insured. The claimant took an assignment and sued the insurer. The insurer argued that the claim was excluded because (1) the insurer's investigation had revealed that the person firing the gun did not fall into the category described by the exception to the exclusion and (2) the claimant had not alleged that the assault and battery was committed while protecting persons or property. Nonetheless, the court ruled that the insurer had breached the duty to defend as a matter of law because the allegations in the complaint did not unambiguously exclude the possibility that the facts could fit within the exception to the exclusion.

The duty to defend is separate and distinct from the insurer's duty to pay a judgment rendered against the insured.[60]

---

[57] *Nationwide Mut. Fire Ins. Co. v. Kim*, 294 Ga. App. 548, 551, 5 S.E.2d 517, 520 (2009).

[58] 307 Ga. App. 609, 705 S.E.2d 707 (2011), cert. denied (Sept. 6, 2011).

[59] *Landmark Am. Ins. Co. v. Khan*, 307 Ga. App. 609, 610, 705 S.E.2d 707, 709 (2011), cert. denied (Sept. 6, 2011).

[60] *Yeoman's & Assocs. Agency, Inc. v. Bowen Tree Surgeons, Inc.*, 274 Ga. App. 738, 742, 618 S.E.2d 673 (2005).

The general rule is that, in making a determination of whether to provide a defense, an insurer is entitled to base its decision on the complaint and the policy. The insurer is under no obligation to independently investigate the claims against its insured.[61] A different rule applies, however, when the complaint on its face shows no coverage, and the insured notifies the insurer of factual contentions that would place the claim within coverage.[62] In such a situation, the insurer has an obligation to give due consideration to its insured's factual contentions and to base its decision on "true facts."[63] In order to base its decision on "true facts," the insurer must necessarily conduct a reasonable investigation into the insured's contentions.[64] Requiring such an investigation does not place an unreasonable burden on insurers, especially in light of the availability of the "procedurally safe course" of providing a defense under a reservation of rights and filing a declaratory judgment action to determine its obligations.[65] An insurer who fails to investigate its insured's contentions and refuses a defense will be liable for a breach of the duty to defend if a reasonable investigation at the time would have established the potential for coverage.[66]

§ 5.5   DUTY TO DEFEND / EXHAUSTION OF POLICY LIMITS

Generally, an insurer does not have a continued duty to defend its insured after the insurer has exhausted policy limits by settling multiple claims with the insured's consent, even though there might be additional claims arising from the

---

[61] *Colonial Oil Industries Inc. v. Underwriters Subscribing to Policy Nos. TO31504670 and TO31504671*, 268 Ga. 561, 562, 491 S.E.2d 337 (1997).

[62] *Id.*

[63] *Colonial Oil*, 268 Ga. at 562, citing *Loftin v. United States Fire Ins. Co.*, 106 Ga. App. 287, 296, 127 S.E.2d 53 (1962).

[64] *Id.*, citing *American Motorists Ins. Co. v. Southwestern Greyhound Lines, Inc.*, 283 F.2d 648, 649 (10th Cir.1960).

[65] *Id.*, citing *Richmond v. Georgia Farm Bureau Mut. Ins. Co.*, 140 Ga. App. 215, 219-220, 231 S.E.2d 245 (1976).

[66] *Colonial Oil Indus. v. Underwriters Subscribing to Policy Nos. TO31504670 and TO31504671*, 268 Ga. 561, 562, 491 S.E.2d 337 (1997).

same accident.[67] In *Liberty Mutual Ins. Co. v. Mead Corp.*, the Supreme Court of Georgia held that the insurer had no further duty to defend remaining claims after settling other claims and exhausting policy limits. The insurer had the insured's consent to settle the claims, and the applicable insurance policy was construed to mean that "the duty to defend is limited by the amount of liability coverage afforded by the policy."[68] Similarly, if the insurer exhausts policy limits in good faith settlements of several claims, the insurer need not defend its insured on later-filed claims arising from the same accident.[69] The rule is true even if the insurer mistakenly enters a defense on the later-filed claim, so long as the insurer did not prejudice the insured.[70]

Based on a recent ruling by the Georgia Supreme Court, it remains to be seen whether this rule will hold true if the insurer commences to defend several claims arising out of a single accident without clearly reserving its rights to withdraw its defense at such time as policy limits are exhausted by payment to one or more of the claimants.[71]

"An insurer's duty to defend its insured is not satisfied when the insurer settles by paying its policy limits to the wrong party."[72] The insurance policy in *Atkinson v. Atkinson* (like the one in *Liberty Mutual Ins. Co. v. Mead*), provided that the duty to defend would end upon payment of policy limits. The insurer entered a defense and paid policy limits, but to the wrong party. Because the payment did not resolve the case against the insured, the insurer could not withdraw.

---

[67] *Liberty Mutual Ins. Co. v. Mead Corp.*, 219 Ga. 6, 12, 131 S.E.2d 534 (1963); *Gibson v. Preferred Risk Mutual Ins. Co.*, 216 Ga. App., 871, 873, 456 S.E.3d 248 (1995).

[68] 219 Ga. 6, 9, 131 S.E.2d 534, 536.

[69] *Gibson v. Preferred Risk Mutual Ins. Co.*, 216 Ga. App. 871, 873, 456 S.E.2d 248 (1995).

[70] *Id.*

[71] *World Harvest Church, Inc. v. GuideOne Mut. Ins. Co.*, 2010 WL 1739943 (Ga. 2010).

[72] *Atkinson v. Atkinson*, 254 Ga. 70, 76, 326 S.E.2d 206, 213 (1985).

These cases do not mean, however, that if an insured faces many lawsuits arising from a single accident, and it is clear that the liability will exceed policy limits, the insurer may tender the policy limits into court and withdraw from the defense of the lawsuits.[73] The insurance policy at issue in *Anderson v. U.S. Fid. & Guar. Co.* (like most liability policies) provided that the insurer must defend as well as indemnify. The court ruled that allowing the insurer to tender policy limits into court addresses only the duty to indemnify and constituted a breach of the duty to defend while actions were pending.[74]

When an insurer is faced with a matter involving multiple claimants where the damages may exceed the policy limits, the insurer might take the following steps to reduce its potential bad faith exposure[75]:

(1) reasonably and expediently investigate the matter and "attempt to ascertain the insured's potential liability, identify the claimants, and assess the nature and extent of the claimants' injuries or damages";

(2) "communicate with the insured concerning her potential liability as soon as possible" - inform the insured that the insurer will retain defense counsel and that the insured has the right to retain her own counsel and "diligently attempt to document all communications with its insured";

---

[73] *Anderson v. US Fid. & Guar. Co.*, 117 Ga. App. 520, 339 S.E.2d 660 (1986).

[74] 117 Ga. App. 520, 521, 339 S.E.2d 660, 661.

[75] Douglas R. Richmond, *Too Many Claimants or Insureds and Too Little Money: Insurers' Good Faith Dilemmas*, Tort Trial & Insurance Practice L.J., Spring Summer 2009, 892-896.

(3) "communicate with all claimants to inform them of [the insurer's] policy limits – both per person and per occurrence – and its willingness to exhaust its limits to achieve a global resolution." This may include convening a mediation or settlement conference. "The insurer should set a reasonable time limit for the claimants to accomplish their voluntary allocation. The insurer should also explain that if the claimants cannot reach agreement on the allocation of policy proceeds by the deadline, [the insurer] will either (1) file an interpleader action; or (2) begin settling individual claims as it deems reasonable." An insurer "should carefully document all communications with the various claimants and their counsel. If claimants or their lawyers misstate facts in communications, the insurer should attempt to correct their misimpressions."

(4) "keep the insured apprised of the settlement process and its strategy."

(5) if the claimants cannot reach a resolution amongst themselves, "the insurer should settle with individual claimants in a reasonable manner," attempting to "prioritize the claims that pose the greatest threat of personal liability to the insured."

§ 5.6   DUTY TO DEFEND MULTIPLE INSUREDS

Where there are multiple insureds under a single policy, each insured is entitled to a separate defense.[76] An insurer

---

[76] *Strain Poultry Farms, Inc. v. American Southern Ins. Co.*, 128 Ga. App. 600, 604, 197 S.E.2d 498 (1973).

owes a duty of good faith and fair dealing to each insured.[77] An additional insured, however, may have to elect coverage under the policy by notifying the insurer of his election and demanding a defense.[78]

§ 5.7   RESERVATION OF RIGHTS / WAIVER AND ESTOPPEL

A reservation of rights "is designed to allow an insurer to provide a defense to its insured while still preserving the option of litigating and ultimately denying coverage."[79]   The seminal case on the issue is *Richmond v. Georgia Farm Bureau Mut. Ins. Co.*[80]   In that case, the insured's minor son was driving his father's car when he hit a pedestrian.   Immediately after the accident, the pedestrian was taken to the hospital and the insured volunteered to pay medical expenses.   Eight months after the accident, the insured received a letter from the pedestrian's attorney indicating that suit would be filed.   The insured gave notice to his insurer, who sent the insured a non-waiver agreement.   The insured refused to sign the non-waiver, instead demanding an unqualified defense.   The insurer sent a letter to its insured unilaterally reserving its rights, retained counsel to defend its insured and sought declaratory relief as to coverage.   The Georgia Court of Appeals looked favorably upon the approach used by the insurer, approving of a "reservation of rights letter" that "fairly informs the insured of the insurer's position."[81]

The Georgia Supreme Court has ruled "where...an insurer assumes and conducts an initial defense without effectively

---

[77]   Douglas R. Richmond, *Too Many Claimants or Insureds and Too Little Money: Insurers' Good Faith Dilemmas*, Tort Trial & Insurance Practice L.J., Spring/Summer 2009, 897.

[78]   *Southeastern Stages, Inc. v. General Fire & Cas. Co.*, 151 Ga. App. 487, 488, 260 S.E.2d 399 (1979).

[79]   *Hoover v. Maxum Indem. Co.*, 291 Ga. 402, 405, 730 S.E.2d 413 (2012).

[80]   *Richmond v. Georgia Farm Bureau Mut. Ins. Co.*, 140 Ga. App. 215, 221, 231 S.E.2d 245 (1976).

[81]   *Id.* 140 Ga. App. at 219-220.

notifying the insured that it is doing so with a reservation of rights, the insurer is deemed estopped from asserting the defense of noncoverage regardless of whether the insured can show prejudice."[82]   This opinion impliedly overrules a long line of cases previously holding that the doctrines of waiver and estoppel are not available to bring within the coverage of a policy risks not covered by its terms, or risks expressly excluded.[83]

An insurer that denies coverage and a defense for a specific reason waives the right to deny coverage for other reasons at a later time.[84]   In *Hoover v. Maxum Indem. Co.*, a claimant was injured while working for his employer. The claimant filed a lawsuit, and the insurer denied coverage and refused to defend. In the letter denying coverage, the insurer relied on an Employers Liability Exclusion as the basis for the refusal to defend.[85]   The denial letter stated that it reserved the right to deny coverage for other reasons at a later date. The claimant received a $16.4 million judgment, took an assignment from the insured and filed suit against the insurer. The insurer defended based on the Employers Liability Exclusion as well as late notice. The trial court granted summary judgment for the insurer on the late notice issue, and the Court of Appeals affirmed. The Supreme Court of Georgia reversed, ruling that the insurer had denied all coverage defenses not set forth in the denial of coverage.[86]

An insurer who defends under a proper reservation of rights may withdraw its defense if the investigation reveals non-

---

[82]   *World Harvest Church, Inc. v. GuideOne Mut. Ins. Co.*, 287 Ga. 149, 156, 695 S.E.2d 6 (2010).
[83]   *Danforth v. Government Employees Ins. Co.*, 282 Ga. App. 421, 427, 638 S.E.2d 852 (2006), citing *Sargent v. Allstate Ins. Co.*, 165 Ga. App. 863, 865, 303 S.E.2d 43 (1983).
[84]   *Hoover v. Maxum Indem. Co.*, 291 Ga. 402, 407, 730 S.E.2d 413 (2012).
[85]   291 Ga. at 404, 730 S.E.2d at 415-16.
[86]   *Hoover v. Maxum Indem. Co.* involved a third-party claim under a liability policy. The Court did not address whether the same principle would apply with regard to a denial of coverage under a first-party property policy.

coverage, but the insurer must do so seasonably and not delay its decision.[87] If an insurer learns of information indicating that no coverage exists under the policy, the insurer is
required to inform the insured immediately.[88] In addition,
an insurer who pays the excess of a property damage claim
without a reservation of rights has not waived the defense of
noncoverage where no action had been filed and the insurer
had not undertaken the defense of the insured.[89] An insurer
may also be estopped to deny coverage if the insurer undertakes the defense of the insured and is negligent in its handling of the defense.[90]

Where an insurer seeks rescission of an insurance contract,
the insurer is not authorized to reserve its rights and file a
declaratory judgment action. In *Minnesota Lawyers Mut.
Ins. Co. v. Gordon*[91], Minnesota Lawyers Mutual ("MLM")
issued a liability policy to an attorney who was sued after a
property closing.[92] MLM initially provided a defense to the
insured but reserved its rights under the policies.[93] MLM
then filed a declaratory judgment and amended its complaint several times. On the final amendment, MLM asserted that the insured's policies should be void due to the
insured's alleged misrepresentations in applying for the
policies.[94] The Court of Appeals held that

> While a declaratory judgment is authorized
> when circumstances show a necessity for a de-
> termination of the dispute to guide and protect

---

[87] *Home Indemnity Co. v. Godley*, 122 Ga. App. 356, 361, 177 S.E.2d 105
(1970), citing 7A Appelman, Insurance Law and Practice, § 4693.

[88] *Ponse v. Atlanta Cas. Co.*, 254 Ga. App. 641, 563 S.E.2d 499 (2002).

[89] *Cotton States Mut. Ins. Co. v. State Farm Mut. Auto. Ins.*, 235 Ga. App.
510, 512, 510 S.E.2d 78 (1998).

[90] *Gibson v. Preferred Risk Mut. Ins. Co.*, 216 Ga. App. 871, 873, 456
S.E.2d 248 (1995).

[91] 315 Ga.App. 72, 726 S.e.2d 562 (2012).

[92] *Id.* at 72.

[93] *Id.* at 72.

[94] *Id.* at 73.

the plaintiff from uncertainty and insecurity with regard to the propriety of some future act or conduct, rescission is not characterized by uncertainty. To the contrary, if a party to a contract seeks to avoid it on the ground of fraud or mistake, he must, upon discovery of the facts, at once announce his purpose and adhere to it.[95]

Since MLM took a firm position as to its rights in requesting rescission of the policies, a declaratory judgment was inappropriate.[96]

§ 5.8   NO ACTION CLAUSE

Many policies contain a provision limiting the amount of time in which an insured can bring suit against its insurer, effectively reducing the statute of limitations by way of contractual agreement. Such a contractual limitation or "no-action" clause provides that any suit against the insurer arising out of the policy must be brought within a specific time following "inception of the loss" or some other trigger. Such provisions are generally enforceable.[97] The Supreme Court of Georgia has expressly rejected arguments that such clauses are "unfair," ambiguous when, for example, they are read with other requirements allowing an insurer 60 days to decide on payment after submission of a proof of loss.[98]

---

[95] *Id.* at 74-75.

[96] *Id.* at 76.

[97] *Thornton v. Georgia Farm Bureau Mut. Ins. Co.*, 287 Ga. 379, 381, 695 S.E.2d 642, 643 (2010). See also, *Morrill v. Cotton States Mut. Ins. Co.*, 293 Ga. App. 259, 262, 666 S.E.2d 582 (2008), citing *McCoury v. Allstate Ins. Co.*, 254 Ga. App. 27, 28(1), 561 S.E.2d 169 (2002), *Allstate Ins. Co. v. Sutton*, 290 Ga. App. 154, 157(1), 658 S.E.2d 909 (2008), *Suntrust Mtg. v. Ga. Farm Bureau Mut. Ins. Co.*, 203 Ga. App. 40, 41, 416 S.E.2d 322 (1992), and *Darnell v. Fireman's Fund Ins. Co.*, 115 Ga. App. 367, 154 S.E.2d 741 (1967).

[98] *Thornton v. Georgia Farm Bureau Mut. Ins. Co.*, 287 Ga. 379, 381, 695 S.E.2d 642, 643 (2010).

An insurer may waive the contractual limitation "where the insurer leads the insured by its actions to rely on its promise to pay, express or implied"[99] or where conduct on the part of the insurer reasonably leads the insured to believe that strict compliance with the limitation provision would not be insisted upon.[100] For example, where settlement negotiations lead the policyholder to believe that payment will be forthcoming without a lawsuit, the insurer cannot require the action to be brought within a certain time.[101] Also, if an insurer does not deny liability and takes actions indicating an intent to pay the claim without suit, an issue of fact is presented as to whether the insured was lulled into a belief that the limitation for filing suit was waived.[102] However, "mere negotiation for settlement, unsuccessfully accomplished, is not that type of conduct designed to lull the claimant into a false sense of security so as to constitute a waiver of the limitation defense."[103]

Where suit has been delayed beyond the stipulated time on account of direct promises to pay the claim, the action is not barred by delay.[104] It is not necessary that there be an actual promise to pay in order for the acts of the insurer to effect a waiver of the time limitation if facts show that negotiations for a settlement have led the insured to believe that

---

[99] *Balboa Life & Cas., LLC v. Home Builders Fin., Inc.*, 304 Ga. App. 478, 481, 697 S.E.2d 240, 244 (2010).

[100] *Brown v. Nationwide Ins. Co.*, 167 Ga. App. 84, 84, 306 S.E.2d 62 (1983) citing *General Ins. Co. of America v. Lee Chocolate Co.*, 97 Ga. App. 588, 103 S.E.2d 632 (1958).

[101] *Nee v. State Farm Fire & Cas. Co.*, 142 Ga. App. 744, 747, 236 S.E.2d 880 (1977).

[102] *Balboa Life & Cas., LLC v. Home Builders Fin., Inc.*, 304 Ga. App. 478, 481, 697 S.E.2d 240, 244 (2010) (reversing trial court that ruled that no action clause was waived as a matter of law.

[103] *Georgia Farm Bureau Mut. Ins. Co. v. Pawlowski*, 284 Ga. App. 183, 184, 643 S.E.2d 239, 241 (2007).

[104] *Id.*, citing *Stanley v. Sterling Mut. Life Ins. Co.*, 12 Ga. App. 475, 477, 77 S.E. 664 (1912).

the insurer will pay the claim.[105] In most cases, whether a waiver occurred is a jury issue.[106]

The Georgia Insurance Commissioner has adopted regulations requiring that no-action clauses in certain policies be no less than two years.[107] The Supreme Court of Georgia has ruled that the regulation violated the Commissioner's authority by contradicting O.C.G.A. § 33-32-1(a), providing for a no-action clause of no less than two years for fire insurance policies.[108]

§ 5.9 INSURER'S DUTY TO PROVIDE POLICY INFORMATION

O.C.G.A. § 33-3-28(a)(1) states that:

> Every insurer providing liability or casualty insurance coverage in this state and which is or may be liable to pay all or a part of any claim shall provide, within 60 days of receiving a written request from the claimant, a statement, under oath, of a corporate officer or the insurer's claims manager stating with regard to each known policy of insurance issued by it, including excess or umbrella insurance, the name of the insurer, the name of each insured, and the limits of coverage. Such insurer may provide a copy of the declaration page of each such policy in lieu of providing such information.

In order to trigger the insurer's duty, the claimant's request must set forth under oath the specific nature of the claim asserted and must be mailed by certified mail or statutory

---

[105] *Id.*

[106] *Id.* (citations omitted).

[107] Ga. Comp. R. & Regs. 120-2-20-.01. The Georgia Insurance Commissioner has the authority to make and enforce regulations to implement the insurance code. *See* O.C.G.A. § 33-2-9.

[108] *White v. State Farm Fire & Cas. Co.*, 291 Ga. 306, 728 S.E.2d 685 (2012).

overnight delivery.[109] The insurer must amend the information provided upon discovery of facts inconsistent with or in addition to the information provided.[110]

Providing information as required by this Code section does not waive the insurer's coverage defenses and is not admissible in evidence unless otherwise admissible under Georgia law.[111] The statute is directive only; it does not create a cause of action and right of a claimant to seek damages if an insurer fails to comply with the statute.[112] However, an insurer's failure to disclose limits can give rise to claims for misrepresentation, false swearing, fraud, and RICO violations, and courts have upheld damages for fraud where the insurer failed to disclose limits in response to a valid request.[113] An insurer may not charge the requesting claimant for the expense involved in complying with a request for information pursuant to O.C.G.A. § 33-3-28.[114]

§ 5.10 INSURED'S DUTY TO COOPERATE

Most policies contain a "cooperation clause" that requires an insured to cooperate with the insurer in the investigation and defense of a claim.[115] More specifically, the insured must cooperate in the insurer's investigation, attend trial and make "full, fair, complete and truthful disclosures of the facts known to him relative to the [incident] when called

---

[109] O.C.G.A. § 33-3-28(a)(1).

[110] O.C.G.A. § 33-3-28(d).

[111] O.C.G.A. § 33-3-28(c).

[112] *Parris v. State Farm Mut. Auto. Ins. Co.*, 229 Ga. App. 522, 524, 494 S.E.2d 244 (1997); *Generali-U.S. Branch v. Southeastern Sec. Ins. Co.*, 229 Ga. App. 277, 280, 493 S.E.2d 731 (1997).

[113] *See Merritt v. State Farm*, 247 Ga. App. 442, 544 S.E.2d 180 (2000); *Parris*, 229 Ga. App. at 526 ("[I]t is not a universal truth in insurance disclosure matters that all is well that ends well. Improper insurance reporting may result in liability under a proper factual scenario.").

[114] Op. Atty. Gen. No. U90-10 (May 7, 1990).

[115] *H.Y. Akers & Sons, Inc. v. St. Louis Fire & Marine Ins. Co.*, 120 Ga. App. 800, 802, 172 S.E.2d 355 (1969).

upon to do so."[116] If an insurer's investigation includes an examination under oath of the insured, and the insured completely fails to appear at the examination under oath, that failure could preclude recovery under the policy.[117]

If the insured willfully and intentionally fails to cooperate, and this failure is prejudicial to the insurer in the defense or settlement of a claim, the insurer is relieved of the duty to defend or indemnify the insured for any judgment the insurer would be required to pay under the policy.[118]

> The insurer must show: (a) that it reasonably requested its insured's cooperation in defending against the plaintiff's claim, (b) that its insured willfully and intentionally failed to cooperate, and (c) that the insured's failure to cooperate prejudiced the insurer's defense of the claim...Once the insurer presents evidence that it was entitled to withdraw coverage, the burden shifts to the plaintiff to establish that the insured's failure to cooperate was justified.[119]

However, if the insured's non-cooperation is merely technical or inconsequential, the insurer is generally not relieved of its duties.[120] The insurer has the burden of proving that it diligently sought to obtain the insured's cooperation and that the insured willfully and intentionally failed to cooper-

---

[116] *St. Paul Fire & Marine Ins. Co. v. Gordon,* 116 Ga. App. 658, 660, 158 S.E.2d 278 (1967).

[117] *Firemen's Fund Ins. Co. v. Sims,* 115 Ga. 939, 42 S.E. 269 (1902).

[118] *Hurston v. Georgia Farm Bureau Mut. Ins. Co.,* 148 Ga. App. 324, 325, 250 S.E.2d 886 (1978).

[119] *Vaughan v. ACCC Ins. Co.,* 314 Ga.App. 741, 742-743, 725 S.E.2d 855 (2012).

[120] *H.Y. Akers & Sons, Inc. v. St. Louis Fire & Marine Ins. Co.,* 120 Ga. App. 800, 802, 172 S.E.2d 355 (1969).

ate.[121] If the insurer makes a showing of diligence and good faith, the burden shifts to the insured to show that his failure to cooperate was excused or justified.[122]

If an insured voluntarily fails to attend trial after receiving a request to do so, the insured's actions are generally considered *per se* prejudicial to the insurer.[123] The insured's total failure to cooperate may preclude recovery under the policy as a matter of law. However, if the insured cooperates to some degree or provides an explanation for non-compliance, the insured's failure to cooperate becomes a jury issue.[124] The insured has a duty to keep up with his case and has a duty to reply to communications addressed to him by or on behalf of the company regarding his claim.[125] At the same time, the insurer has a duty to keep its insured informed once it has taken over the handling of the claim or lawsuit against its insured.[126]

---

[121] *Allstate Ins. Co. v. Hamler*, 247 Ga. App. 574, 577, 545 S.E.2d 12 (2001), citing *Diamonds & Denims v. First of Ga. Ins. Co.*, 203 Ga. App. 681, 683, 417 S.E.2d 440 (1992).

[122] *H.Y. Akers & Sons, Inc. v. St. Louis Fire & Marine Ins. Co.*, 120 Ga. App. 800, 804, 172 S.E.2d 355 (1969) ("The insurer has the burden of showing a violation of the [cooperation] clause by the insured, and he who seeks to enforce a claim against the insurer under the policy has the burden of refuting the affirmative defense, once *prima facie* made, by evidence of justification or excuse. To show a *prima facie* breach the insurer is required to do no more than show that it exercised good faith and diligence in an effort to procure the attendance of the insured at the trial and that he did not attend.").

[123] *Id.* 120 Ga. App. at 803, 172 S.E.2d 355 (1969), citing *Glens Falls Indemnity Co. v. Keliher*, 88 N.H. 253, 187 A. 473, 476-477 (1936) and *Beam v. State Farm Mutual Auto. Ins. Co.*, 269 F.2d 151, 154 (6th Cir. 1959) ("Every person familiar with the trial of cases by jury knows that the case of an individual defendant is seriously, if not hopelessly, prejudiced by his absence from the trial. His failure to be present in defense of the claim can have an intangible effect upon the jury both as to the question of liability and the amount of the verdict, the net effect of which is difficult to measure. Unexpected developments in the plaintiff's evidence might be offset by an explanation on the part of the insured.").

[124] *Allstate Ins. Co. v. Hamler*, 247 Ga. App. 574, 577, 545 S.E.2d 12 (2001), citing *Diamonds & Denims v. First of Ga. Ins. Co.*, 203 Ga. App. 681, 683, 417 S.E.2d 440 (1992).

[125] *H.Y. Akers & Sons, Inc. v. St. Louis Fire & Marine Ins. Co.*, 120 Ga. App. 800, 804-805, 172 S.E.2d 355 (1969).

[126] *Springer v. Citizens Cas. Co. of N.Y.*, 246 F.2d 123, 128 (5th Cir. 1957) (insurer has a duty to keep insured reasonably informed of the facts as disclosed by its investigation).

Finally, an insured violates the cooperation clause by collusively assisting maintenance of the claimant's suit rather than assisting the insurer.[127]

§ 5.11 UNFAIR CLAIMS PRACTICES ACT

Georgia's Unfair Claims Settlement Practices Act is designed "to set forth standards for the investigation and disposition of claims arising under policies or certificates of insurance issued to residents of Georgia."[128] The UCSPA does not cover claims involving workers' compensation, fidelity, or surety insurance.[129] The Act sets out fourteen acts that constitute unfair claims settlement practices when committed (1) flagrantly and in conscious disregard of the insurance laws of the State of Georgia or (2) with such frequency so as to indicate a general business practice to engage in such conduct.[130] An insurer commits an unfair claims settlement practice by:[131]

(1) Knowingly misrepresenting to claimants and insureds relevant facts or policy provisions relating to coverages at issue;

(2) Failing to acknowledge with reasonable promptness pertinent communications with respect to claims arising under its policies;

(3) Failing to adopt and implement procedures for the prompt investigation and

---

[127] *Hurston v. Georgia Farm Bureau Mut. Ins. Co.*, 148 Ga. App. 324, 325, 250 S.E.2d 886 (1978), *citing Elliott v. Met. Cas. Ins. Co. of New York*, 250 F.2d 680, 684 (10th Cir. 1957), *cert denied*, 356 U.S. 932, 78 S.Ct. 774, 2 L.Ed.2d 762 (1958).

[128] O.C.G.A. § 33-6-31.

[129] *Id.*

[130] O.C.G.A. § 33-6-34; O.C.G.A. § 33-6-33.

[131] O.C.G.A. § 33-6-34.

settlement of claims arising under its policies;

(4) Not attempting in good faith to effectuate prompt, fair, and equitable settlement of claims submitted in which liability has become reasonably clear;

(5) Compelling insureds or beneficiaries to institute suits to recover amounts due under its policies by offering substantially less than the amounts ultimately recovered in suits brought by them;

(6) Refusing to pay claims without conducting a reasonable investigation;

(7) When requested by the insured in writing, failing to affirm or deny coverage of claims within a reasonable time after having completed its investigation related to such claim or claims;

(8) When requested by the insured in writing, making claims payments to an insured or beneficiary without indicating the coverage under which each payment is being made;

(9) Unreasonably delaying the investigation or payment of claims by requiring both a formal proof of loss and subsequent verification that would result in duplication of information and verification appearing in the formal proof of loss form; provided, however, this paragraph shall not preclude an insurer from obtaining sworn statements if permitted under the policy;

(10) When requested by the insured in writing, failing in the case of claims denial or

offers of compromise settlement to provide promptly a reasonable and accurate explanation of the basis for such actions. In the case of claims denials, such denials shall be in writing;

(11) Failing to provide forms necessary to file claims within 15 calendar days of a request with reasonable explanations regarding their use;

(12) Failing to adopt and implement reasonable standards to assure that the repairs of a repairer owned by the insurer are performed in a workmanlike manner;

(13) Indicating to a first-party claimant on a payment, draft check, or accompanying letter that said payment is final or a release of any claim unless the policy limit has been paid or there has been a compromise settlement agreed to by the first-party claimant and the insurer as to coverage and amount payable under the contract; and

(14) Issuing checks or drafts in partial settlement of a loss or claim under a specific coverage which contain language which releases the insurer or its insured from its total liability.

There is no private right of action under the Georgia UCSPA.[132] Rather, the Georgia Insurance Commissioner enforces the UCSPA.[133] Despite the fact that an insured

---

[132] O.C.G.A. § 33-6-37; *Rodgers v. St. Paul Fire & Marine Ins. Co.*, 228 Ga. App. 499, 502, 492 S.E.2d 268 (1997), citing O.C.G.A. § 33-6-37; *Burgess v. Allstate Ins. Co.*, 334 F. Supp. 2d 1351, 1364 (N.D. Ga. 2003).

[133] O.C.G.A. § 33-6-35.

cannot raise a cause of action under the UCSPA, an insured may attempt to use evidence of a violation of the Act as evidence of an insurer's bad faith. Courts routinely admit evidence of a state's unfair claim practices act and regulations in insurance bad faith actions.[134]

---

[134] *See, e.g., Ingalls v. Paul Revere Life Ins. Co.*, 561 N.W.2d 273 (N.D. 1997) (violation of state's Prohibited Practices in Insurance Business Act may be considered as evidence of bad faith); *Walston v. Monumental Life Ins. Co.*, 923 P.2d 456, 461 (Idaho 1996) (expert witness testimony on insurance statute proper to show insurance industry standards even though no private cause of action exists under the statute); *Spray, Gould & Bowers v. Associated International Ins. Co.*, 71 Cal. App. 4th 1260, 84 Cal. Rptr. 552 (Cal. App.1999) (court looks to insurance regulations to determine if there was a violation of a duty that estops insurer from raising certain defense); *MacFarland v. United States Fidelity & Guarantee Co.*, 818 F. Supp. 108, 110 (E.D. Pa. 1993) (unfair claim practices act and regulations can be considered in determining whether insurer engaged in bad faith); *Certainteed Corp. v. Federal Ins. Co.*, 913 F. Supp. 351 (E.D. Pa. 1995) (allowed evidence of unfair claims practices act and regulations to be considered in determining whether insurer engaged in bad faith); *Weiford v. State Farm Mutual Automobile Ins. Co.*, 831 P.2d 1264, 1269 (Ala. 1992) (where insured had common law bad faith claim no error in instructing on duties imposed by unfair claim practices act); *Inland Group of Cos., Inc. v. Providence Washington Ins.* Co., 985 P.2d 674, 683 (Idaho1999) (upholding use of expert testimony to "utilize Idaho's Unfair Claims Settlement Practices Act to show insurance industry practices in Idaho"); *Rottmund v. Continental Assurance Co.*, 813 F. Supp. 1104 (E.D. Pa.1992) (courts may look to other statutes upon the same or similar subjects to define bad faith); *Coyne v. Allstate Ins. Co.*, 771 F. Supp. 673, 678 (E.D. Pa.1991) (provisions of UIPA can be utilized to describe conduct constituting bad faith); *Wailua Associates v. Aetna Casualty & Surety Co.*, 27 F.Supp.2d 1211, 1221 (D. Hawaii 1998) ("the Court finds that violations of the unfair settlement provision...may be used as evidence to indicate bad faith").

CHAPTER 6

ETHICAL ISSUES IN INSURANCE PRACTICE

§ 6.1 THE "TRIPARTITE RELATIONSHIP"

When a liability insurer retains defense counsel to represent an insured, the resulting relationship among the three parties is often called a "tripartite relationship."[1] This relationship is unique in the insurance context.[2] Georgia, like a majority of states, generally holds that the defense attorney has two clients: the insurance company and the insured.[3] In most situations, the objectives of the insurer and the insured align and the tripartite relationship is beneficial to all parties. Insurers have an interest in controlling the costs of litigation, which can be done through billing arrangements with appointed counsel. In turn, defense attorneys receive regular business from their insurance company clients and are generally well compensated for their services. Meanwhile, the insured is to be provided a defense from competent counsel with expertise in defending against claims brought against the insured.

Nonetheless, any time multiple parties are involved in such a relationship, ethical issues arise. One court stated that

---

[1] *See, e.g., General Sec. Ins. Co. v. Jordan, Coyne & Savits, LLP*, 357 F. Supp. 2d 951, 956 (E.D. Va. 2005) (citing cases) ("Although most of the reported cases involving [the question whether an insurer can bring a legal malpractice claim against the law firm it retains to defend an insured] offer no analysis of the insurer's relationship with the law firm, the few that do reflect the view that a 'tripartite relationship' exists among insurer, insured, and counsel, with both insurer and insured as co-clients of the firm in the absence of a conflict of interest."). Some jurisdictions hold that an insurer has a direct attorney-client relationship with the attorney it retained to represent its insured. *See, e.g., Hartford Ins. Co. of Midwest v. Koeppel*, 629 F. Supp. 2d 1293, 1299 (M.D. Fla. 2009) (citing cases).

[2] William G. Passannante and Diana Shafter Gliedman, *On the Horns of a Defense Counsel Dilemma: Insurance Conflicts Counsel Can Help Avoid Losing Your Coverage*, The Corporate Counselor (January 2, 2008).

[3] Formal Advisory Opinion 86-4 (Georgia Supreme Court, 1987) (noting that "the attorney for the insured is also the attorney for the insurer").

the ethical dilemma created by the tripartite relationship would "tax Socrates, and no decision or authority ... furnishes a completely satisfactory answer."[4]   Lawyers appointed by the insurance company may be in-house attorneys, staff counsel, "captive" law firms, or panel counsel. Regardless of the label, the attorney appointed by the insurance company to represent the insured typically has a business or employment relationship (often a long-standing one) with the insurer.   The laws of human nature attendant to this relationship are difficult to ignore.

> Even the most optimistic view of human nature requires us to realize that an attorney employed by an insurance company will slant his efforts, perhaps unconsciously, in the interest of his real client – the one who is paying his fee and from whom he hopes to receive future business – the insurance company.[5]

The close relationship between defense counsel and the insurance company is often a concern of both insureds and the courts.[6]

As made clear below, the best practice for avoiding conflict issues in the "tripartite relationship" is prediction of such conflicts and communication when they appear on the horizon.   Counsel could and should evaluate possible ethical issues at the inception of each representation.   As issues arise, the Georgia Rules of Professional Conduct and Formal Advisory Opinions issued by the Georgia Supreme Court address aspects of the tripartite relationship.   Where the Georgia

---

[4] *Hartford Acc. & Indem. Co. v. Foster*, 528 So.2d 255, 273 (Miss. 1988).

[5] Robert E. O'Malley, *Ethics Principles for the Insurer, the Insured, and Defense Counsel: The Eternal Triangle Reformed*, 66 Tul. L. Rev. 511, 515 (1991).

[6] Richmond, Douglas R., *Lost in the Eternal Triangle of Insurance Defense Ethics*, 9 Georgetown Journal of Legal Ethics 475, 482 (1996) ("Most insurance defense attorneys have an on-going relationship with their insurers, and they work hard at developing future business. Conversely, few defense attorneys enjoy continuing relationships with the insureds they are hired to represent. It is this strong and perpetual economic linkage between insurers and their regular counsel that most concerns courts and insureds.").

Rules do not address the issues, attorneys should look to the Model Rules of Professional Conduct and the Formal and Informal Advisory Opinions of the American Bar Association (ABA). With such guidance in mind, the following addresses some common concerns presented by the tripartite relationship.

§ 6.2   WHO IS THE CLIENT?

An attorney owes a duty of loyalty to his or her client. This duty is expressed in the obligations to exercise independent professional judgment on behalf of the client, and to decline representation or withdraw if the ability to do so is adversely affected by the representation of another client.[7] An attorney who does not know to whom his highest loyalty should be given – who his client is – is bound to drift into ethical trouble.[8]

In a typical insurance case where coverage is not contested, a policyholder is involved in a potentially covered incident. The insured tenders the claim to its insurer and requests a defense. The insurer retains defense counsel to defend the insured. However, in a case where the interests of the insured and the insurer diverge, to whom does the attorney's duty of loyalty extend? Courts take several different views of whether defense counsel represents the insurer, the insured, or both. These views are called the "two-client", "one-client", and "third-party payor" (or "one-and-a-half client") theories.

---

[7]   Formal Advisory Opinion 05-13 (Georgia Supreme Court, 2007). See also Georgia Rule of Professional Conduct 1.7, Comments 1-4.

[8]   May, David N., *Inhouse Defenders of Insureds: Some Ethical Considerations*, 46 Drake L. Rev. 881, 904 (1997-1998).

(a)   Two-client theory.

A majority of courts hold that the lawyer has two clients: the insurance company and the insured.[9] Courts that adopt this theory reason that both the insured and the insurer are beneficiaries of the insurance company's exclusive control over the litigation.[10] These courts also recognize that, in general, "companies and insureds usually enjoy a substantial commonality of interests, even when their interests do not perfectly align."[11]

In Georgia, whether a lawyer represents a party is a question of fact, not appearances, unless the party knowingly caused the attorney to appear as his agent in that matter.[12] Georgia has not officially adopted the two-client rule in case law, although the Georgia Supreme Court's Formal Advisory Opinion 86-4 notes "the attorney for the insured is also the attorney for the insurer"[13]. There may be some circumstances where defense counsel's duty to the insured makes the insured the "primary" client. The Opinion addresses the "ethical propriety of the plaintiff's attorney in a personal injury case writing a letter to the insured defendant which may contain legal advice."[14] The Supreme Court stated that the appropriate attorney to provide advice regarding the insured's legal rights is the insured's attorney. A potential conflict arises because both the insured and the insurer are the defense counsel's clients.[15] Interestingly, the Supreme

---

[9]   Nathan Andersen, *Risky Business: Attorney Liability In Insurance Defense Litigation – A Review of the Arizona Supreme Court's Decision in Paradigm Insurance Co v. Langerman Law Offices*, 2002 BYU L. Rev. 643, 665 citing cases).

[10]   *Id.* at 665-666.

[11]   *Id.* at 666, *quoting* Charles Silver, *Does Insurance Defense Counsel Represent the Company or the Insured?*, 72 Tex. L. Rev. 1583, 1609 (1994).

[12]   *Pembroke State Bank v. Warnell*, 218 Ga. App. 98, 102 (Ga. Ct. App. 1995) citing *Addley v. Beizer* 205 Ga. App. 714, 718, 423 S.E.2d 398 (1992), quoting *20/20 Vision Center v. Hudgens*, 256 Ga. 129, 134, 345 S.E.2d 330 (1986).

[13]   *Supra*, n.3.

[14]   *Id.*

[15]   *Id.*

Court appears to switch from a "two-client" theory to a "one-client" theory, stating: "the dilemma is only apparent. [Defense counsel] represents the insured as a client and has a duty to keep the insured fully informed by virtue of the rules of ethics...[Defense counsel] has a duty to inform the insured not only of any offer of settlement...but also of the potential liability of the insurer for a bad faith refusal to accept any reasonable offer within the policy limits."[16]

(b)   One-client theory.

Although still the minority view, there is an increasing judicial trend toward holding that defense counsel's only client is the insured.[17]

In *Atlanta International Ins. Co. v. Bell*[18], the Michigan Supreme Court held that no attorney-client relationship existed between an insurance company and defense counsel. Atlanta filed a malpractice suit against the attorneys that it retained to represent Atlanta's insured in a premises liability case, claiming that the attorneys failed to raise a particular defense.[19] Whether Atlanta had the standing to sue the attorneys depended upon the existence of an attorney-client relationship between the insurer and the attorneys it hired to represent the insured.[20] Stating that "courts have consistently held that the defense attorney's primary duty of loyalty lies with the insured, and not the insurer," the court

---

[16] *Id.* See also *Mead Corp. v. Liberty Mut. Ins. Co.*, 107 Ga. App. 167, 171, 129 S.E.2d 162 (1962), rev'd with respect to insurer's duty to defend by *Liberty Mut. Ins. Co. v. Mead Corp.*, 219 Ga. 6, 131 S.E.2d 534 (1963) ("Attorneys, whether or not paid by insurance companies, owe their primary obligation to the insured they are employed to defend...")

[17] *Id.* at 666, *citing* Eileen M. Dacey, *The Delicate Balance of the Attorney-Client Privilege in the Tripartite Relationship*, 602 PLI/LIT 199, 205 (1999). Additionally, The language of the Restatement (Third) of the Law Governing Lawyers appears to demonstrate the American Law Institute's preference for the one-client theory.

[18] 438 Mich. 512, 475 N.W.2d 294 (1991) (plurality opinion).

[19] *Id.* at 296.

[20] *Id.*

allowed the insurer to proceed pursuant to the doctrine of equitable subrogation.[21] The court noted that

> To hold that an attorney-client relationship exists between insurer and defense counsel would indeed work mischief, yet to hold that a mere commercial relationship exists would work obfuscation and injustice. The gap is best bridge by resort to the doctrine of equitable subrogation to allow recovery by the insurer. Equitable subrogation best vindicates the attorney-client relationship and the interests of the insured, properly imposing the social costs of malpractice where they belong. Allowing the insurer to stand in the shoes of the insured under the doctrine of equitable subrogation best serves the public policy underlying the attorney-client relationship.[22]

(c)   Third-party payor theory.

The third-party payor or "one-and-a-half client" theory "advocates that 'the lawyer be deemed to represent both the insurer and the insured until something goes wrong, at which point the insurer would no longer be a client, at least in the usual sense."[23] The theory considers that the insurer is often in the best position to manage and control the litigation, but relies on the attorney to protect its economic interests. If the attorney can do so without compromising the loyalty the attorney owes to the insured, then the insurer also owes a duty of care to the insurer. Since the insurer relies upon the attorney's representation of the insured, the insurer is per-

---

[21]   *Id.* at 297-298.

[22]   *Id.* at 297.

[23]   Andersen, 2002 BYU L. Rev. 643, *citing* Nancy J. Moore, *The Ethical Duties of the Insurance Defense Lawyer: Are Special Solutions Required?* 4 Conn. Ins. L. J. 259, 276 (1997-98).

mitted to insure the attorney who acts negligently.[24]   It is important to note, though, that although this theory allows insurers control over the costs of litigation, the control is limited and insurers are not necessarily able to enjoy the full range of benefits or rights of control that they desire.[25]

§ 6.3   SITUATIONS IN WHICH POTENTIAL ETHICAL ISSUES ARISE

(a)   Providing a defense when the insurer reserves its rights.

The most common problem that arises in the "tripartite relationship" occurs when the carrier undertakes the defense of the insured pursuant to a reservation of rights. In such cases, it is possible for an insurer to take less interest in paying for a vigorous defense, because the insurer may ultimately prevail on the coverage issue and withdraw its defense. Additionally, if defense counsel is aware of the coverage issues, defense counsel may gather discovery or steer the case toward a coverage result that is favorable to the insurer (for example, by eliciting deposition testimony that supports a particular coverage defense).[26]   In these cases, conflicts can generally be avoided where (1) appointed defense counsel withdraws or (2) the insured is allowed to select independent counsel.[27]

When defending under a reservation of rights, the insurer should not hire attorneys who provided the coverage opinion as defense counsel for the insured. Instead, independent defense counsel with no involvement in the coverage issue should be appointed to avoid the conflict.

---

[24] *Id*. at 668.
[25] *Id*. at 669.
[26] Richmond, Douglas R., *Walking a Tightrope: The Tripartite Relationship Between Insurer, Insured, and Insurance Defense Counsel*, 73 Neb. L. Rev. 265, 272-273 (1994).
[27] *Id*. at 273.

(b)   Damages Exceed Coverage Available Under the Policy.

In a case where an insured has a solid liability defense but the claimed damages exceed policy limits, conflicts arise for defense counsel. An insurer may want to aggressively litigate a case in hopes of receiving a defense verdict or a judgment below policy limits. Such a course of action puts at risk the insured's personal assets, because a plaintiff's verdict may result in a judgment in excess of policy limits. The defense attorney may find herself in a conflicting situation, where settling is in the best interest of the insured client, but the insurer may think twice about continuing a business relationship with a defense attorney who is unwilling to try hard cases.[28] In addition, defense counsel may be personally liable for failing to settle within the policy limits.[29] This conundrum can create the need to hire separate, independent defense counsel to represent the interests of the insured. Similar conflicts may arise where the insured has a self-insured retention (SIR) that requires the insured to bear the first dollars of loss (insurance is excess over the SIR). The SIR may apply to defense costs as well as judgments or settlements.[30]

In claims where the damages may exceed the policy limits, defense counsel should be on the lookout for "conflict clues" – signs that clients have unusual interests that must be protected.[31] One of these signs is the existence of the excess exposure itself, as the insured may have uninsured assets at

---

[28]   *Id*. 73 Neb. L. Rev. at 278-279.
[29]   *Id*. 73 Neb. L. Rev. at 278-279, citing *Mutuelles Unies v. Kroll & Linstrom*, 957 F.2d 707 (9th Cir. 1992) ($2 million malpractice judgment verdict against a law firm representing the insured where the plaintiff in the underlying action demanded $1 million to settle but trial counsel refused to offer more than $900,000).
[30]   Pryor, Ellen S. and Charles Silver, *Defense Lawyer's Professional Responsibilities: Part I – Excess Exposure Cases*, 78 Tex. L. Rev. 599, 618 (1999-2000).
[31]   *Id*. at 659.

risk and have an unusually strong interest in the outcome.[32] Another "conflict clue" is a request from one client to persuade another client of the merits of a particular course of action, such as when an insured requests that the defense lawyer pressure the carrier to accept a demand within the policy limits.[33]

Defense counsel should conspicuously inform the insured of the risk of a judgment in excess of policy limits and advise the insured of the right to retain independent coverage counsel.[34] Of course, merely informing the insured of the right to retain independent counsel does not relieve the insurer of the duty to act in good faith.[35]

(c)   Eroding Limits and Exhaustion of Limits.

Although policy limits generally constitute the boundaries of the insurer's indemnity obligations, most liability policies do not limit the amount an insurer must pay in defense of claims. One way an insurer may limit defense costs and its overall exposure is through the use of "eroding" or "burning limits" policies.[36] In these policies, defense costs erode indemnity limits. In other words, every dollar spent on defense reduces by one dollar the amount available to settle or otherwise resolve the claim.[37] Increasing numbers of professional liability policies and employment practices liability policies include eroding limits. Although the idea is gaining popularity among automobile, homeowners' and commercial

---

[32] *Id.*

[33] *Id.*

[34] *Id.* 73 Neb. L. Rev. at 287.

[35] *See Smoot v. State Farm Mut. Auto. Ins. Co.*, 299 F.2d 525, 531-532 (11th Cir. 1962) ("Smoot II").

[36] Brandon, David L., *Burning Issues*, Los Angeles Lawyer, April 2004, at 30. "Burning limits" policies may also be referred to as "wasting," "cannibalizing,", "self-consuming," or "defense within limits" policies. *Id.* at 30, citing *Rus, Milband & Smith v. Conkle & Olesten*, 113 Cal.App. 4th 656, 661 n.1 (2003) and Wayne Baliga, *Insurance Law; Understanding the ABC's*, 652 PLI/Lit 463, 477 (2001).

[37] Brandon, Los Angeles Lawyer, April 2004, at 30.

general liability policies,[38] competitive markets in some industries and state regulations are likely to curtail expansive use of eroding coverage.

A similar situation arises when there are several claims, and the payment of one or more exhausts policy limits. Whether an insurer has a duty to continue to defend its insured after policy limits have been exhausted is a contractual matter spelled out in the policy.[39] Depending on the policy and the use of the limits, an insurer's duty to defend some claims may be satisfied by defending and accomplishing a good-faith settlement of other claims in a manner that provides a real benefit to the insured.[40]

In either situation, defense counsel must advise the insured of the benefits of a suggested litigation activity (for example, hiring an expensive expert) and its potential effect on both the defense of the case and the available indemnity limits.[41] In doing so, however, the defense attorney must be careful not to give coverage advice. In his or her initial letter to the insured regarding undertaking the defense assignment, the defense attorney should specifically state that he or she will not be rendering any coverage advice.[42]

It is good practice for an attorney handling a defense pursuant to a declining limits policy is for the attorney to create a liability analysis report and a litigation budget as soon as possible. These tools should be updated regularly, with cop-

---

[38] *Id.*

[39] *Liberty Mut. Ins. Co. v. Mead Corp.*, 219 Ga. 6, 8, 131 S.E.3d 534 (1963); *Scruggs v. International Indemnity Co.*, 233 Ga. App. 772, 773, 505 S.E.2d 267 (1998).

[40] *See, Liberty Mut. Ins. Co. v. Mead Corp.*, 219 Ga. 6, 12, 131 S.E.3d 534 (1963); *Gibson v. Preferred Risk Mut. Ins. Co.*, 216 Ga. App., 871, 873, 456 S.E.3d 248 (1995).

[41] Brandon, Los Angeles Lawyer, April 2004, at 32, citing Shaun McParland Baldwin, *Legal and Ethical Considerations for "Defense within Limits" Policies*, 61 Def. Couns. J. 89, 99 (1994).

[42] Brandon, Los Angeles Lawyer, April 2004, at 36, n.9.

ies sent to the insurer and the insured. An attorney who
determines that potential defense costs may impair the insurer's ability to indemnify the insured for exposure should
bring that issue to both the insurer and the insured's attention as early as possible.[43]

In dealing with plaintiff's counsel, the best course of action
is to be candid about the fact that the policy limits may be
reduced by defense costs. In a 2003 case in California, the
Court of Appeal found that an insured's judgment creditor
could sue the attorney who had been retained by the insurer
to provide a coverage analysis when that attorney misrepresented the scope of coverage available for the claim.[44]

When policy limits are exhausted, insurers generally advise
their insured and defense counsel that the insurer will no
longer be funding the defense. However, an insurer's decision to cease payment does not end the defense attorney's
duty to the client. Counsel must follow the prescribed rules
for withdrawing from cases.[45] It is not clear whether exhaustion of policy limits in and of itself allows a defense attorney to seek an order of withdrawal. A court may hold
that an attorney who undertakes the defense of an insured
under a burning limits policy does so at his own peril and
with knowledge that there is a maximum amount available
for defense costs.[46] Some courts have refused to allow an
attorney to withdraw from representation when the insurer
ceased to pay for the defense.[47]

---

[43] Brandon, Los Angeles Lawyer, April 2004, at 32.
[44] Brandon, Los Angeles Lawyer, April 2004, at 32, *citing Shafer v. Ber-
ger, Kahn, Shafton, Moss, Figler, Simon & Gladstone*, 107 Cal. App. 4th 54, 74
(2003).
[45] *See* Georgia Rule of Professional Conduct 1.16.
[46] Brandon, Los Angeles Lawyer, April 2004, at 33.
[47] *Id.* citing *Smith v. Anderson-Tulley Co.*, 608 F. Supp. 1143 (S.D. Miss
1985), *aff'd*, 846 F.2d 751 (5th Cir. 1988) (federal court refused to permit an attorney to withdraw from representation of an insured even though the insurer
claimed that payment of policy limits ended its duty to defend) and *Heller v. Alter*,
257 N.Y.S. 391 (N.Y. 1932) (court held that mere fact that insurer was unable to

Ethical issues arise for the plaintiff's attorney as well. A plaintiff's attorney, in gathering policy information at the outset of litigation, should attempt to determine whether the policy is an eroding limits policy. Obviously, in a declining limits policy, amounts spent on aggressive litigation decrease the plaintiff's potential recovery.[48] As part of initial litigation strategy, a plaintiff's attorney should weigh the pros and cons of conducting certain activities (such as extensive discovery) and consider how those activities may bear on the ultimate recovery. The plaintiff's attorney should also disclose these issues to the client and explain how certain litigation tactics may impact recovery.[49]

(d)   Multiple Insureds.

Where multiple insureds are entitled to a defense under the same policy for the same claim, the insurer often assigns the same defense counsel to defend the insureds, creating potential conflicts. For example, a passenger in a car may sue both the driver and the owner of the car after a wreck. An owner and a driver are typically entitled to a defense under the same policy. However, the driver and the owner may have conflicting interests if, for example, the owner asserts that the driver was operating the car without permission.[50]

If hired to represent multiple insureds under the same policy, defense counsel should, at the inception of the representation (1) analyze the potential conflicts among the insureds; (2) disclose these potential conflicts in writing to each insured and the insurer; and (3) obtain valid conflict waivers from all parties.[51] Even after these initial disclosures, defense counsel should continue to monitor potential conflicts,

---

fund the defense did not relieve defense counsel of an obligation to continue representing the insured).

[48]   Brandon, Los Angeles Lawyer, April 2004, at 32.
[49]   *Id.* (citations omitted).
[50]   Richmond, 73 Neb. L. Rev. at 279.
[51]   Richmond, 73 Neb. L. Rev. at 295-296.

as they may ultimately require defense counsel to withdraw.[52]

(e)   Coverage Defenses.

Georgia Rule of Professional Conduct 1.6(a) states:

> A lawyer shall maintain in confidence all information gained in the professional relationship with a client, including information which the client has requested to be held inviolate or the disclosure of which would be embarrassing or would likely be detrimental to the client, unless the client consents after consultation, except for disclosures that are impliedly authorized in order to carry out the representation, or are required by these rules or other law, or by order of the Court.

In the course of a representation of an insured, defense counsel may learn of information supporting a coverage defense. Regardless of whether the attorney learns of the information through independent investigation and activities, or whether the insured informs the attorney of the information, defense counsel is generally barred from disclosing the information to the insurer.[53]

A famous case illustrating this conflict is *Parsons v. Continental National American Group*.[54] The Parsons were violently assaulted by Michael Smithey, the 14-year-old son of CNA's insureds. CNA appointed counsel to defend the Smitheys in the resulting lawsuit. During the lawsuit, the attorney informed CNA of a confidential file on Michael Smithey from a psychiatric institution that treated him. Counsel reported that the confidential file showed that the boy knew what he was doing was wrong. Counsel further reported to the insurer that "the assault [Michael] commit-

---

[52]   Richmond, 73 Neb. L. Rev. at 296.
[53]   Richmond, 73 Neb. L. Rev. at 281.
[54]   550 P.2d 94 (Ariz. 1976).

ted on claimants can only be a deliberate act on his part."
After receiving this letter, CNA sent a reservation of rights
to the Smitheys warning that Michael's act might have been
an intentional act excluded from coverage. In preparation
for trial, defense counsel interviewed Michael and wrote to
CNA: "[Michael's] own story makes it obvious that his acts
were willful and criminal." At trial, the court granted the
Parson's motion for a directed verdict on the issue of Michael's liability, and a judgment was entered against him for
$50,000.

The Parsons then garnished the CNA policy and offered to
settle for the limits of $25,000. CNA rejected the offer. In-
stead, CNA defended the garnishment action by claiming
that the intentional acts exclusion applied. The same law
firm and attorney that had represented Michael represented
CNA in the garnishment action. The Parsons contended
that CNA was estopped to deny coverage and had waived
the intentional acts exclusion because the company exploited
the relationship between its appointed defense counsel and
the Smithey's son. The Arizona Supreme Court agreed. After noting that defense counsel obtained confidential and
privileged information by virtue of the attorney-client relationship:

> [W]e hold that such conduct constitutes a waiver of
> any policy defense, and is so contrary to public policy
> that the insurance company is estopped as a matter of
> law from disclaiming liability under any exclusionary
> clause in the policy.

Accordingly, CNA was liable for the entire $50,000 judg-
ment.

Three years before *Parsons*, the Texas Supreme Court held
that an insurer was estopped from denying coverage due to
the insured's late notice where the defense counsel hired by
the insurance company to represent the insured "actively
work[ed] against [the insured] in developing evidence for

[the insurer] on the coverage question."[55]   The Texas Supreme Court stated that "[a]n attorney employed by an insurer to represent the insured simply cannot take up the cudgels of the insurer against the insured..."[56] An attorney's actions against his client in this manner violates the rules of professional conduct.   An attorney should not act as both defense counsel for the insured and coverage counsel for the insurer.

(f)   Non-Covered Claims, Counterclaims and
         Third-Party Actions.

In some cases, defense counsel may become aware that the insured has a potential counterclaim against another party in the lawsuit or a third-party claim that may be barred if not asserted in the pending action. Insurance policies do not necessarily provide coverage for these additional claims, and the insurer will not pay the defense attorney to prosecute them. The proper course of action for the defense attorney is to advise the insured (1) of the existence of such claims; (2) that the insurance policy may not provide coverage for the prosecution of such claims; and (3) that the insured may wish to consult counsel at his own expense with regard to such claims.[57] When an insured expresses a desire to pursue a counterclaim, defense counsel may be obligated to fully protect those interests without regard to the language of the insurance policy.   This obligation may arise as a consequence of the attorney's duty to represent his client zealously and within the bounds of the law.

(g)   Punitive Damages.

Some insurance policies exclude punitive damages. If the complaint otherwise triggers the duty to defend, a conflict

---

[55] *Employers Casualty Co. v. Tilley*, 496 S.W.2d 552, 554. (Tex. 1973). This case was cited in the *Parsons* opinion.

[56] *Id.* at 560.

[57] Richmond, 73 Neb. L. Rev. at 288.

arises between the insurer and insured. The insurer may have little interest in defending the punitive damages claim, as the insurer might have no duty to indemnify the insured for that aspect of damages. If an insurer is not obligated to indemnify its insured for punitive damages, it may attempt to limit defense counsel's activities with regard to defending that aspect of the claim. At the outset of the representation of a punitive damages case, defense counsel must determine whether the policy provides coverage for punitive damages and advise both the insured and the insurer of punitive damages claims so that they may protect their respective interests.[58] In any event, the defense attorney must continue to defend the punitive damage claims.

(h)   Settlement within Policy Limits.

Defense counsel has a duty to keep the insured client fully informed of all settlement negotiations.[59] In Formal Advisory Opinion 86-4, the Georgia Supreme Court cited *Rogers v. Robson, Masters, Ryan, Brumund & Belom*, an Illinois case involving an insurer's settlement over the express objection of the insured.[60] Dr. James Rogers was sued for negligence by a patient. Dr. Rogers' malpractice insurer provided a defense. During discovery, deposition testimony established that Dr. Rogers was not negligent. The malpractice policy provided that written consent of the insured was not required before the insurer settled any claim or suit. Despite Dr. Rogers' express instructions not to settle, defense counsel negotiated a settlement. Dr. Rogers then brought suit against the attorneys. In opposition to the law firm's motion for summary judgment, Dr. Rogers filed an affidavit in which he stated that he repeatedly informed one of the partners that he would not consent to a settlement, that he was assured the action would be defended, and that

[58]   Richmond, 73 Neb. L. Rev. at 282-283.
[59]   Formal Advisory Opinion 86-4.
[60]   *Rogers v. Robson, Masters, Ryan, Brumund & Belom*, 81 Ill. 2d 201, 407 N.E. 2d 47 (1980).

the attorneys never advised him that they intended to settle the suit.

In affirming denial of summary judgment for the law firm, the Supreme Court of Illinois noted that when the attorneys became aware that settlement was imminent and that Dr. Rogers did not want to settle the case, a conflict of interest arose that prevented the attorneys from continuing to represent both Dr. Rogers and the insurer without full disclosure. The attorneys breached their duty to Dr. Rogers and were liable for any damages stemming from the breach. The Supreme Court of Illinois then stated:

> Although [the attorneys] were employed by the insurer, [Dr. Rogers], as well as the insurer, was their client and was entitled to a full disclosure of the intent to settle the litigation without his consent and contrary to his express instructions. [The attorneys'] duty to make such disclosure stemmed from their attorney-client relationship with [Dr. Rogers] and was not affected by the extent of the insurer's authority to settle without [Dr. Rogers'] consent. We need not and therefore do not consider the question whether [Dr. Rogers'] insurance carrier was authorized to settle the malpractice action without his consent. Further, since no disclosure was made and [Dr. Rogers] was not given the opportunity to elect what course to pursue, we need not speculate on what recourse, if any, [Dr. Rogers] had under the terms of the insurance policy.

When faced with a situation where the insured and the insurer disagree on a settlement strategy, defense counsel can require the parties to work out disagreements on their own.[61] Defense counsel can provide an objective assessment of the likely out-

---

[61]   78 Tex. L. Rev. at 660.

come at trial and estimate future defense costs. Defense counsel can also encourage the clients to obtain separate counsel or a mediator. However, defense counsel should refrain from making an "all things considered" settlement recommendation without obtaining informed waivers from the insured and the insurer.[62]

> (i)   "Advice" to the Defendant from Plaintiff's Counsel.

Ethical issues may arise when an insurer refuses an offer to settle within policy limits, and the plaintiff's counsel writes a letter to the insured defendant regarding the matter. In Formal Advisory Opinion No. 86-4, the Supreme Court of Georgia first stated the general rules that an insurer is normally only liable for the portion of a judgment that is within the policy limits; the insured is liable for any portion of the judgment that is in excess of those limits; an insurer may have a duty to settle a claim within policy limits under the "equal consideration" rule; and failure to do so may subject the insurance company to liability for a judgment in excess of policy limits.[63]

The plaintiff's attorney is clearly prohibited from directly contacting an insured defendant who is represented by counsel.[64] Thus, such a letter to an insured defendant represented by counsel is "impermissible." The Supreme Court laid the task of informing the insured of his or her rights against the insurer squarely on the shoulders of the insured's attorney:

> The appropriate attorney for this purpose [to inform the insured of his or her rights] is the insured's attor-

---

[62] *Id.* at 660.

[63] Formal Advisory Opinion 86-4 (12/17/87), citing *National Emblem Ins. Co. v. Pritchard*, 140 Ga. App. 350, 231 S.E.2d 126 (1976); *United States Fidelity & Guaranty Co. v. Evans*, 116 Ga. App. 93, 156 S.E.2d 809, *aff'd* 223 Ga. 789, 158 S.E.2d 243 (1967); *State Farm Ins. Co. v. Smoot*, 381 F.2d 331 (5th Cir. 1967).

[64] Ga Rule Professional Conduct 4.2(a).

ney. The problem here, of course, is that the attorney for the insured is also the attorney for the insurer...The lawyer representing the insured and the insurer thus faces an apparent dilemma. *But the dilemma is only apparent. He or she represents the insured as a client and has a duty to keep the insured fully informed by virtue of the rules of ethics...*The lawyer for the insurer has a duty to inform the insured not only of any offer of settlement...but also of the potential liability of the insurer for a bad faith refusal to accept any reasonable offer within the policy limits.[65]

(j)   Insurance Fraud.

If an insured engages in fraud (for example, arson) and the defense attorney becomes aware of the fraud, several ethical rules come in to play. Obviously, defense counsel cannot assist or advise an insured that is engaging in such conduct.[66] If an attorney knows that the client is engaging in fraud, the attorney must withdraw from the representation.[67] If an attorney withdraws due to an insured's fraud, the attorney cannot disclose the fraud to the insurer.[68] However, the attorney can give notice of the withdrawal and

---

[65] Formal Advisory Opinion 86-4 (emphasis added).

[66] Georgia Rule of Professional Conduct 1.2(d) ("A lawyer shall not counsel a client to engage in conduct that the lawyer knows is criminal or fraudulent, nor knowingly assist a client in such conduct...").

[67] Georgia Rule of Professional Conduct 1.16(a)(1) ("...a lawyer shall not represent a client or, where representation has commenced, shall withdraw from the representation of a client if (1) the representation will result in violation of the Georgia Rules of Professional Conduct or other law...") and 1.16(b) ("...a lawyer may withdraw from representing a client if withdrawal can be accomplished without material adverse effect on the interests of the client, or if: (1) the client persists in a course of action involving the lawyer's services that the lawyer reasonably believes is criminal or fraudulent; (2) the client has used the lawyer's services to perpetrate a crime or fraud; (3) the client insists upon pursuing an objective that the lawyer considers repugnant or imprudent...").

[68] Georgia Rule of Professional Conduct 1.6.

"may also withdraw or disaffirm any opinion, document, af-
firmation, or the like."[69]

§ 6.4   ETHICAL ISSUES ARISING FROM INSURERS' COST-CONTAINMENT STRATEGIES

(a)   Insurer's Use of Litigation Guidelines.

Many insurers issue to defense counsel "litigation guidelines," which state under what circumstances defense counsel may decide to take certain actions in the defense and under what circumstances prior authorization from the insurer
is necessary.   Georgia Rule of Professional Conduct 1.7(a)
provides as follows: "A lawyer shall not represent or continue to represent a client if there is a significant risk that
the lawyer's own interests or the lawyer's duties to another
client, a former client, or a third person will materially and
adversely affect the representation of the client, except as
permitted [by client consent]."   Where an insurer uses litigation guidelines to control defense costs by limiting defense
counsel's actions in defending the case, Rule 1.7 comes into
play.   For example, guidelines may limit the discovery to be
propounded on adverse parties.   Such restrictions create potential conflicts of interest if they inhibit an attorney's ability to adequately defend a case or interfere with the attorney's independent professional judgment.[70]   For instance, the
Montana Supreme Court has held that Montana attorneys
may not follow an insurer's billing and practice rules which
limit or direct the scope and extent of the attorney's representation of the insured.[71]

---

[69]   Georgia Rule of Professional Conduct 1.6, Comment 14.
[70]   Richmond, 73 Neb. L. Rev. at 283.
[71]   Randall, Susan, *Managed Litigation and the Professional Obligations of Insurance Defense Lawyers*, 51 Syracuse L. Rev. 1, 2-3, n.7 (2001), citing *In Re Rules of Prof'l Conduct & Insurer Imposed Billing Rules & Procedures*, 2 P.3d 806 (Mont. 2000).

The American Bar Association addressed the issue of litigation guidelines in Formal Opinion 01-421.[72] The ABA stated:

> Pursuant to the liability insurance contract, the in-
> sured delegates to the insurance company the right to
> defend the case and is required to cooperate in the in-
> sured's defense. However, the rules of professional
> conduct – and not the liability insurance contract –
> govern the lawyer's ethical obligations to his client,
> whether the client is the insured, the insurer, or both.

As soon as the matter is assigned, the defense attorney
should inform the insured of any limitations on the representation. ABA Formal Opinion 01-421 states:

> If the lawyer is hired to defend an insured pursuant
> to an insurance policy that authorizes the insurer to
> control the defense, and in its sole discretion, to settle
> within policy limits, the lawyer must communicate
> these limitations on his representation of the insured
> to the insured, preferably early in the representation.
> The lawyer should "make appropriate disclosures suf-
> ficient to apprise the insured of the limited nature of
> his representation as well as the insurer's right to
> control the defense in accordance with the terms of
> the insurance contract ... No formal acceptance or
> written consent is necessary. The insured manifests
> consent to the limited representation by accepting the
> defense offered by the insurer after being advised of
> the terms of the representation being offered."[73]

---

[72] In January 1999, the Georgia State Bar proposed Formal Advisory
Opinion Request No. 99-R2, addressing the issue of whether defense counsel could
ethically comply with an insurer's detailed billing guidelines. On September 17,
2001, the Georgia Supreme Court issued a one-line opinion disapproving of the
request as submitted.
[73] ABA Formal Opinion 01-421 (2001), citing ABA Formal and Informal
Ethics Opinions 1983-1998 at 406-407. The ABA noted that in Formal Opinion
96-403, it stated that a lawyer could satisfy the requirements of Rule 1.2(c) by
sending the insured a short letter clearly apprising the insured "of the limitations

The attorney should provide written notice to the insured at the time of retention that:

(1) the attorney has been hired by the insurance company to defend the insured regarding the claim;

(2) the insurance company assumes the defense subject to the terms and conditions of the applicable policy (but the attorney should not make any comment on the terms of coverage or provide any coverage advice);

(3) the insurer has the right to control the defense in accordance with the terms of the insurance policy;[74]

(4) the insurer provides certain guidelines to its defense attorneys regarding the handling of litigation;

(5) the attorney intends to proceed with the defense at the direction of the insurer and within the insurer's guidelines;

(6) the attorney is subject to legal and ethical duties under Georgia law (and explain those duties, such as the duty to maintain confidences);

(7) the insured has the right to obtain his own counsel at his own expense, and that the defense at-

---

of the representation being offered by the insurer and that the lawyer intends to proceed in accordance with the directions of the insurer." [Note: ABA Model Rule of Professional Conduct 1.2(c) and Georgia Rule of Professional Conduct 1.2 (c) are slightly different. Georgia RPC 1.2(c) states: "[a] lawyer may limit the objectives of the representation if the client consents after consultation." ABA Model Rule 1.2(c) states: "A lawyer may limit the scope of the representation if the limitation is reasonable under the circumstances and the client gives informed consent."].

[74] ABA Formal Opinion 96-403 (1996) ("If the lawyer is to proceed with the representation of the insured at the direction of the insurer, the lawyer must make appropriate disclosure sufficient to apprise the insured of the limited nature of his representation as well as the insurer's right to control the defense in accordance with the insurance contract.").

torney will work with that counsel at the insured's direction;

(8) if the insured disagrees with the insurer's conduct of the defense, the insured may refuse the defense offered and proceed with his own counsel at his own expense.

The insured can agree at the outset that his appointed attorney should follow the insurer's direction and does not have to specifically consent to each act or decision that his attorney makes.[75] If the insured disagrees, however, the attorney must follow the wishes of his insured client, to whom he owes his primary duty.[76]

(b)   Outside Auditors.

Insurers sometimes audit defense counsel's fee bills as a cost control measure. A billing audit "encompasses a range of services, from an examination of the face of the legal bill for improper charges or errors to a detailed analysis of original time records, attorney work product, expenses and hourly rate benchmarks, and more."[77] Audits examine hourly rates, background information about the legal matter and lawyer work product to gauge quality, tactics, strategy and performance in context.[78] Ethical problems arise when bills

---

[75] ABA Formal Opinion 96-403 (August 2, 1996) ("As long as the insured is clearly apprised of the limitations on the representation being offered by the insurer and that the lawyer intends to proceed in accordance with the directions of the insurer, the insured has sufficient information to decide whether to accept the defense offered by the insurer or to assume responsibility for his own defense at his own expense. No formal acceptance or written consent is necessary. The insured manifests consent to the limited representation by accepting the defense offered by the insurer after being advised of the terms of the representation being offered. Once the lawyer has apprised the insured of the limited nature of his representation and that he intends to proceed in accordance with the directions of the insurer, he has satisfied the requirements of Rule 1.2(c).").

[76] *Mead Corp. v. Liberty Mut. Ins. Co.*, 107 Ga. App. 167, 171, 129 S.E.2d 162 (1962) ("Attorneys, whether or not paid by insurance companies, owe their primary obligation to the insured they are employed to defend...").

[77] ABA Formal Opinion 01-421 (2001), citing John Toothman, *Surviving a Legal Bill Audit*, 15 Compleat Lawyer 45 (Winter 1998).

[78] *Id.*, citing Toothman, *supra* at 49.

contain confidential or privileged information. Billing records and underlying documentation may reveal the motive of the client in seeking representation, litigation strategy, or the specific nature of the services provided to the insured – information that is generally protected by confidentiality rules, attorney-client privilege, or both.[79] Disclosure of the information required to perform an audit may be particu- larly problematic when coverage issues exist, as work product by defense counsel could harm the insured's interests with regard to the coverage issue.

Formal Opinion 01-421,[80] addresses ethical obligations when an insurer instigates a third-party audit. The opinion states: "A lawyer may not...disclose the insured's confiden- tial information to a third-party auditor hired by the insurer without the informed consent of the insured." In general, defense counsel may inform the insurer about the litigation through periodic status reports, detailed billing statements and the submission of other information, which usually ad- vances the interests of both the insured and the insurer in the representation. These disclosures are impliedly author- ized to carry out the representation.[81] However, a lawyer may not disclose the insured's confidential information to a third-party auditor designated by the insurer without the insured's informed consent.[82] The attorney should advise the insured in writing as to:

---

[79]   ABA Formal Opinion 01-421 (2001).

[80]   In January 1999, the Georgia State Bar proposed Formal Advisory Opinion Request No. 99-R2, addressing the issue of whether defense counsel could ethically comply with an insurer's request that the attorney submit bills to an outside auditor. On September 17, 2001, the Georgia Supreme Court issued a one-line opinion disapproving of the Request as submitted.

[81]   ABA Formal Opinion 01-421 (2001).

[82]   ABA Formal Opinion 01-421 (2001), noting that a majority of jurisdic- tions have concluded that it is not ethically proper for a lawyer to disclose billing information to a third-party billing review company at the request of an insurance company unless he has obtained the client's consent.

(1) the nature of the information sought;

(2) the legal and non-legal consequences of the client's decision to disclose or not disclose the information;

(3) the extent of his obligation under the insurance policy to authorize disclosures to third parties;

(4) consequences of consenting or not consenting to disclosure where the insurance policy requires the insured to cooperate in the defense of the claim and where failure to agree to disclosure could risk loss of coverage;

(5) the fact that the insurer may interpret the "duty to cooperate" clause in its policy as meaning that the insurer has the right to disclose confidential information to third-party contractors; and

(6) the risk that the information disclosed to the auditor could be obtained by others directly or indirectly as a result of the disclosure, the risk that a disclosure could involve a waiver of the attorney-client privilege, and the risk that the disclosure could be used to the insured's disadvantage.[83]

The attorney must respond to the auditor's requests in a manner that safeguard's the client's interests, including minimizing the extent to which information relating to the representation is disclosed to the auditor and avoiding (if possible) disclosures that could result in a waiver of the attorney-client privilege (for example, by redacting certain descriptive portions of fee bills).[84]

---

[83] ABA Formal Opinion 01-421 (2001).
[84] *Id.*

(c)   Defense of an Insured by Insurer's In-House Counsel.

A trend toward the use of in-house counsel to defend insureds has emerged.[85] Insurers benefit because in-house attorneys become specialists not only in general insurance law, but also in the particular workings of their employer. Additionally, the insurer recognizes savings through not paying outside counsel bills.[86]

When an in-house attorney represents an insured, unique ethical issues may arise, including whether the attorney is assisting the insurer in the unauthorized practice of law.[87] The North Carolina Supreme Court held that "a licensed attorney who is a full-time employee of an insurance company [may not] ethically represent one of the company's insureds as counsel of record" as doing so would constitute aiding the insurer in the unauthorized practice of law.[88] There is little doubt that the use of in-house attorneys should intensify attention on the tripartite relationship. However, the majority of jurisdictions – including Georgia – hold that an in-house attorney may defend an insured without engaging the insurer in the unauthorized practice of law.[89]

The ABA has also endorsed this view, holding that the ethics rules do not prevent insurance staff counsel from defending policyholders. Staff counsel for the insurer may provide legal representation to both the insured and insurer in an insurance defense claim, so long as he or she (1) informs the in-

---

[85]   46 Drake L. Rev. 881 at 882.

[86]   *Id.* at 884-885.

[87]   *Id.* at 887-888.

[88]   *Gardner v. North Carolina State Bar*, 316 N.C. 285, 286, 341 S.E.2d 517 (N.C. 1986). The Supreme Court of Kentucky reached the same result in *American Ins. Ass'n v. Kentucky Bar Ass'n*, 917 S.W.2d 568 (Ky. 1996).

[89]   See, e.g., *Coscia v. Cunningham*, 250 Ga. 521, 299 S.E.2d 880 (1983); *Unauthorized Practice of Law Committee v. American Home Assurance Company, et al.*, 261 S.W.3d 24, 43-44 (Tex. 2008) (citing cases).

sured of their status and (2) exercises independent professional judgment.[90]   However, insurance staff counsel must disclose his or her employment status and affiliation with the insurance company to all insureds-clients. Such disclosure should occur at the earliest opportunity, such as during the initial meeting with the client or through appropriate language in the initial letter to the client.[91]

Unique ethical situations arise when an in-house attorney represents an insured. A lawyer employed or retained by an organization represents the organization acting through its duly authorized constituents.[92]   The in-house attorney must ensure that he or she does not develop an attorney-client relationship with an employee of the company who is not a "duly authorized constituent."

An in-house attorney for an insurer must also beware of ethical duties in attorney-client relationships with the insurer's agents as the actions of an agent may have an important (and possibly determinative) impact on an insurer's liability.[93]   For example, an in-house attorney may interview an insurance agent in order to defend a case. If, during that interview, the agent reveals confidential information to the attorney, the attorney may be obligated to maintain the confidentiality of that information. Additionally, if the attorney provides legal advice to the agent, an attorney-client relationship may develop.[94]

---

[90]   ABA Comm. On Ethics and Prof'l Responsibility, Formal Opinion 03-430 (2003).

[91]   *Id.*

[92]   Georgia Rule of Professional Conduct 1.13(a).

[93]   46 Drake L. Rev. at 916-917.

[94]   *Id.* at 917.

CHAPTER 7

NEGLIGENT PROCUREMENT

§ 7.1   INSURANCE AGENTS AND BROKERS

An insurance agent is an individual appointed or employed by an insurer who sells, solicits, or negotiates insurance, or an individual insurance producer.[1] Agents are licensed by and subject to regulation by the state.[2] An agent may be an independent agent, representing at least two insurance companies and serving clients by searching the market for the most coverage at the best price. An agent generally receives a commission and a fee for handling the insured's policy.[3] A captive agent is a representative of a single insurer or group of insurers who is obliged to submit business only to that company, or at the very minimum, give that company first refusal rights on a sale. In exchange, that insurer usually provides its captive agents with an allowance for office expenses as well as an extensive list of employee benefits such as pensions, life insurance, health insurance, and credit unions.[4]

The terms "agent" and "broker" are now often used interchangeably. Early case law suggests that an "agent" usually refers to a captive agent and a "broker" to an independent agent.[5] Here, however, we will use "agent" to refer to both independent and captive agents.

---

[1]   O.C.G.A. § 33-23-1(3) and (10). Sometimes, a party who does not appear to be an agent at first glance may in fact be one. For example, the Court of Appeals has held that an employer, in doing such acts as are necessary to obtain coverage of his employees under a group policy issued to him, to keep the policy of force and to effectuate its purposes, is the agent of the insurance company rather than the insureds. *Cason v. Aetna Life Ins. Co.*, 91 Ga. App. 323, 328, 85 S.E.2d 568 (1954).

[2]   O.C.G.A. § 33-23-1 et seq.

[3]   A.M. Best Glossary of Insurance Terms, available at http://www.ambest.com/resource/glossary.html.

[4]   *Id.*

[5]   *See, e.g., National Indem. Co. v. Berry*, 136 Ga. App. 545, 548-549, 221 S.E.2d 624 (1975) (citations omitted) ("Ordinarily an insurance agent represents

§ 7.2   SCOPE OF AGENT'S AUTHORITY

The general law of agency applies to insurance agents.[6] Under general agency law, a principal is bound by all acts of its agent within the scope of the agent's authority.[7] The express or actual authority of an agent is often spelled out in an agency agreement executed between the insurance company and the agent.

The principal is also bound when the agent lacks express authority but possesses apparent authority.[8] An agent's authority may be established by the principal's conduct and course of dealing. If a principal holds another out as his agent, indicating by his course of dealing that the agent has certain authority, and induces another to deal with his agent pursuant to that apparent authority, the principal is estopped to deny the agent's authority.[9] The acts of the agent which create apparent authority may include written or spoken words or any other conduct of the principal which, reasonably interpreted, causes the third person to believe that the principal consents to have the act done on his behalf by the person purporting to act for him.[10] To prove apparent or ostensible agency, a party must show: (1) the apparent principal represented or held out the apparent agent as

---

the company...whereas an insurance broker represents insured...An insurance agent during his employment sustains a fixed and permanent relation to the company he represents; he is clothed with general powers, and assumes responsibilities not conferred on, or assumed by, a broker; and he owes a duty and allegiance to the company employing him, and seeks patronage only for the profit and benefit of such company and is precluded from soliciting insurance business for others; whereas an insurance broker, as generally understood, owes no duty or allegiance to any particular corporation.")

[6] *Patriot Gen. Ins. Co. v. Millis*, 233 Ga. App. 867, 869, 506 S.E.2d 145 (1998).

[7] O.C.G.A. § 10-6-51.

[8] *Home Materials, Inc. v. Auto Owners Ins. Co.*, 250 Ga. 599, 601, 300 S.E.2d 139 (1983).

[9] *Id.* at 601, *citing Equitable Credit Corp. v. Johnson*, 86 Ga. App. 844, 847, 72 S.E.2d 816 (1952).

[10] *OMNI Builders Risk, Inc. v. Bennett*, 313 Ga. App. 358, 361, 721 S.E.2d 563 (2011), *citing International Indem. Co. v. Odom*, 174 Ga. App. 6, 7(2), 329 S.E. 2d 307 (1985) (citations and punctuation omitted).

having authority and (2) the party's justifiable reliance upon the representation led to the injury.[11] "Apparent authority is not predicated on whatever a third party chooses to think an agent has the right to do, or even upon what the agent says he can do, but must be based on acts of the principal which have led the third party to believe reasonably the agent had such authority."[12] Agency will not be found where the only evidence of that agency is the mere assumption by one party that such agency exists.[13]

(a)   Notice.

Issues of an independent agent's apparent authority often arise when an insured gives notice of a claim or suit to his agent, expecting that notice to the agent to constitute notice to the insurer. As discussed below, independent insurance agents are often considered agents of the insured under Georgia law, and not agents of the insurer.[14] However, an insurer could place an independent insurance agent in a position of apparent authority such that one might be justified in assuming that the agent had authority to receive notice of an occurrence or claim.[15] When the terms of the policy or instructions stamped upon the face of a liability policy instruct the insured that he is to provide notice of suit, either to the independent insurance agent or the insurer, that delegation of apparent authority will estop the insurer to deny any notice that was given to the independent agent under its instructions.[16]

---

[11]   *Kinard v. Nat'l Indem. Co.*, 225 Ga. App. 176, 178-179, 483 S.E.2d 664 (1997), *citing Kirby v. Northwestern Nat'l Cas. Co.*, 213 Ga. App. 673, 678(2), 445 S.E.2d 791 (1994).

[12]   *Rutland v. State Farm Mut. Auto. Ins. Co.*, 426 Fed. Appx. 771, 775-776 (11th Cir. 2011), *citing Thompson v. Gen. Motors Acceptance Corp.*, 193 Ga. App. 740, 741, 389 S.E.2d 20 (1989) (quotation marks omitted).

[13]   *Kinard, supra* at 179, *citing* Howard v. St. Paul Fire & Marine Ins. Co., 180 Ga. App. 802, 804, 350 S.E.2d 776 (1986).

[14]   *Southeastern Express Systems v. Southern Guar. Ins. Co.*, 224 Ga. App. 697, 700, 482 S.E.2d 433 (1997).

[15]   *Kay-Lex Co. v. Essex Ins. Co.*, 286 Ga. App. 484, 489, 649 S.E.2d 602 (2007), *citing Southeastern Express, supra* at 700.

[16]   *Southeastern Express, supra* at 700.

In *International Indem. Co. v. Odom*[17], the Court of Appeals considered the question of an agent's authority to receive notice on behalf of an insurer. The policy delivered to the insured stated that in the event of an accident, the insured should "notify your agent or Alexander Underwriters, Inc." The insured had applied for his policy through the George H. Greene Insurance Agency, Inc. ("Greene"), made all payments on his insurance to Greene and only had contact with the insurer through Greene.[18] The insured was injured in an accident, and the insured's wife gave notice of the accident to Greene before the insured left the hospital (the insured suffered brain damage as a result of the accident and he was unable to give notice on his own.) The insurer claimed that notice was insufficient because Greene was an independent broker rather than an agent of the insurer.[19] The Court of Appeals disagreed, noting that "[a]pparent authority to do an act is created as to a third person by written or spoken words or any other conduct of the principal which, reasonably interpreted, causes the third person to believe that the principal consents to have the act done on his behalf by the person purporting to act for him."[20] The Court of Appeals further stated that when a principal places a purported agent in a position of apparent authority so that a person of ordinary prudence is justified in assuming that the agent has authority to perform a particular act, and deals with the agent accordingly, the principal is estopped from denying the agency.[21] By stating on the policy that the insured could "notify [Greene] or Alexander Underwriters, Inc." the insurer placed Greene in a position of apparent authority and the insured was justified in assuming that Greene had the authority to receive notice of the accident. The Court of Appeals held

---

[17]   174 Ga. App. 6, 6-7, 329 S.E.2d 307 (1985).
[18]   *Id.* at 7.
[19]   *Id.*
[20]   *Id.* (citations omitted).
[21]   *Id* (citations omitted).

that the insurer was estopped to deny that Greene was its agent.[22]

(b)   Knowledge Imputed to Insurer.

Where an insurance company gives an agent the authority (either actual or apparent) to acquire knowledge for the company or to act for the company in issuing a policy, the agent's knowledge as to matters within the general scope of the agent's authority is imputed to the company even if the company attempts to place express limitations on the power of that agent.[23]

(c)   Waiver of Policy Provisions.

An insurance agent generally does not have the power to waive policy provisions unless the agent receives express authority to do so from the insurer.   For example, an insurance agent does not have the authority to waive a policy provision that states that suit must be brought within twelve months of the date of loss.   Absent some fraud by the agent that induces the insured to delay bringing the lawsuit until after the time for bringing suit has expired, the insured cannot rely on the agent's conduct as an excuse for failing to sue in a timely manner.[24]

§ 7.3   DUAL AGENCY

Independent agents or brokers are often considered the agent of the insured.[25]   However, Georgia law recognizes the concept of dual agency, where an agent acts on behalf of

---

[22]   *Id.*

[23]   *New York Life Ins. Co. v. Patten*, 151 Ga. 185, 187, 106 S.E. 183 (1921).

[24]   *Auto-Owners Ins. Co. v. Ogden*, 275 Ga. 565 569 S.E.2d 833 (Ga. 2002), *citing Gibralter Fire & Marine Ins. Co. v. Lanier*, 64 Ga. App. 269, 274-275 (13 S.E.2d 27) (1941).

[25]   *Kirby v. Northwestern Nat'l Cas. Co.*, 213 Ga. App. 673, 678, 445 S.E.2d 791 (1994); *European Bakers, Ltd. v. Holman*, 177 Ga.App. 172, 172(2), 338 S.E.2d 702 (1985).

both the insured and the insurer.[26]   Dual agency is not considered void per se as against public policy in Georgia.[27] Dual agency is proper where the principals have knowledge of the dual agency and do not repudiate it. Dual agency does not in and of itself relieve the agent of responsibility to either of the principals.[28]

Georgia courts take a number of factors into consideration to determine whether a dual agency exists. For example, courts consider:

    (1)   whether the agent is an independent agent or a captive agent;

    (2)   the relationship between the insured and the agent, including the length of the relationship and whether the insured followed the agent if the agent's office changed;

    (3)   how many insurers the agent contacted in order to place coverage for the insured;

    (4)   whether the agency was authorized, by contract or custom, to accept premiums on behalf of the insurer; and

    (5)   whether the agency was authorized, by contract or custom, to accept notice of claims on behalf of the insurer.

When an insurer holds out a person as having the authority to act on its behalf and a third party reasonably relies on that authority, the agent is cloaked with apparent authority.[29] This authority can engender a dual agency. For example, where an agent countersigns insurance policies,

---

[26]   *Sumitomo Marine & Fire Ins. Co. v. Southern Guaranty Ins. Co.*, 337 F.Supp.2d 1339, 1352 (N.D. Ga. 2004), citing cases.

[27]   *Home Materials, Inc. v. Auto Owners Ins. Co.*, 250 Ga. 599, 602, 300 S.E.2d 139 (1983), *citing Spratlin, Harrington & Thomas, Inc. v. Hawn*, 116 Ga. App. 175, 156 S.E.2d 402 (1967).

[28]   *Home Materials, supra* at 602, *citing Wright Body Works v. Columbus Interstate Ins. Agency*, 233 Ga. 268, 210 S.E.2d 801 (1974).

[29]   *Id., supra* at 1353, citing *Kirby, supra* at 678 and *Whitaker v. Zirkle*, 188 Ga.App. 706, 709, 374 S.E.2d 106 (1988).

declaration pages, and certificates of insurance as an "authorized representative" of an insurer, a third party may reasonably believe that the agent has authority to act on behalf of the insurer.[30] A fiduciary relationship may arise between an independent insurance agency and an insurer when the agency customarily accepts premiums and claims on the insurer's behalf.[31] A dual agent's misrepresentations as to the existence of insurance coverage will obligate the insurer to provide coverage.[32]

§ 7.4   LIABILITY OF AGENTS

Generally an insurance company is estopped to deny liability on any matter arising out of the fraud, misconduct, or negligence of an agent of the company. If an applicant gives correct answers or information to an insurance company's agent, and the agent inserts false answers into the application, the insurer is estopped to assert the falsity of those answers.[33] Additionally, if an insured makes a false statement on an application and the insurer's agent has actual knowledge that the statement is false, the agent's knowledge is imputed to the insurer and the insurer is estopped to assert the defense of fraud or misrepresentation.[34]

Under Georgia law, an insurance agent who negligently fails to procure insurance coverage may be liable to the insured for any resulting loss.[35] In some situations, however, if the

---

[30]   *Id.* at 1353.
[31]   *Bowen Tree Surgeons, Inc. v. Canal Indemnity Company*, 264 Ga.App. 520, 523, 591 S.E.2d 415 (2003), *discussing Byrne v. Reardon*, 196 Ga.App. 735, 397 S.E.2d 22 (1990).
[32]   *Auto-Owners Ins. Co. v. Anderson*, 2005 U.S. Dist. LEXIS 47809, *4 (M.D. Ga. Feb. 10, 2005), *citing Home Materials, Inc. v. Auto-Owners Ins. Co.*, 250 Ga. 599, 300 S.E.2d 139 (1983).
[33]   *Patriot Gen. Ins. Co. v. Millis*, 233 Ga. App. 867, 869-870 (1998), *citing Stillson v. Prudential Ins. Co. of America*, 202 Ga. 79, 82, 42 S.E.2d 121 (1947).
[34]   *Jones v. United Ins. Co.*, 177 Ga. App. 102, 103 (1985), *citing Reserve Life Ins. Co. v. Bearden*, 96 Ga. App. 549, 101 SE2d 120 (1957).
[35]   *Turner, Wood & Smith, Inc. v. Reed*, 169 Ga. App. 213, 214, 311 S.E.2d 859 (1983) ("Generally speaking, an insurance agent who undertakes to procure a

insured is provided with a copy of the policy and the contents of the policy plainly show that the agent did not procure what was requested, the agent may be insulated from liability.[36] Exceptions apply when, for example, the agent has a fiduciary-like relationship with the insured or performs expert services on behalf of the insured under circumstances in which the insured must rely upon the expertise of the agent to identify and procure the correct amount or type of insurance.[37] For example, a small business was relieved of the responsibility to minutely examine its policy to determine if the coverage required was included in the terms of the policy where the business's agent held itself out as an expert in the field of insurance. The agency examined the business's records and the business requested that the agency obtain a sufficient amount of business interruption insurance to properly protect the business. The agent further undertook to review the business audits annually and to determine if such policies continued to be sufficient. In doing so, the agency did more than simply issue a policy – it acted as an expert advisor to the business.[38] This exception applies where the prospective insured must rely on the expertise of the agent to identify and procure the correct amount or type of insurance.[39] By contrast, where an insured specifically

---

policy of insurance for his principal but negligently fails to do so may be held liable to the principal for any resulting loss.") *See also Carrollton Fed. S. & L. Assn. v. Young*, 165 Ga. App. 262, 299 SE2d 395 (1983); *Holyoak v. Houston-Gaskins Agency*, 160 Ga. App. 565, 287 SE2d 572 (1981); *Speir Ins. Agency v. Lee*, 158 Ga. App. 512, 281 SE2d 279 (1981); *Northeastern Ins. Agency v. Courson*, 156 Ga. App. 321, 322-323, 274 SE2d 714 (1980).

   [36] *Atlanta Women's Club, Inc. v. Washburne*, 207 Ga.App. 3, 4, 427 S.E.2d 18 (1992) ("Atlanta Women's Club I"), *citing Turner, Wood & Smith v. Reed*, 169 Ga.App. 213, 214, 311 S.E.2d 859 (1983) and *Ethridge v. Associated Mutuals*, 160 Ga.App. 687, 688, 288 S.E.2d 58 (1981).

   [37] *Atlanta Women's Club, Inc. v. Washburne*, 207 Ga.App. 3, 4-5, 427 S.E.2d 18 (1992) ("Atlanta Women's Club I") (citations omitted). See also *Stillwell v. Allstate Ins. Co.*, 663 F.3d 1329, 1333-34 (11th Cir. 2011) (explaining that "there are at least two exceptions to this rule regarding the insured's obligation to read the policy").

   [38] *Wright Body Works v. Columbus Interstate Ins. Agency*, 233 Ga. 268, 271, 210 S.E.2d 801 (1974).

   [39] *Epps v. Nicholson*, 187 Ga. App. 246, 248(2), 370 S.E.2d 13 (1988).

requests a certain kind of coverage, giving the agent no discretion in the type of insurance to be procured, the exception might not apply.[40] Whether an insurance agent performed expert services or exercised expert discretion in procuring the requested coverage will necessarily vary depending on the unique facts and circumstances of each case.[41]

The insured is not relieved of *all* responsibility to read the policy. The duty to read remains where an examination of the policy would have made it readily apparent that the coverage contracted for was not issued.[42] As an insurance policy is to be read as a layman would read it and not as an insurance expert might analyze it, it must be readily apparent to a layman reading the insurance policy, based upon the plain and ordinary meaning of clear and unambiguous language, that the risk causing the loss was not covered.[43]

§ 7.5   LIMITATION ON DAMAGES

An insurance agent's bad faith may be imputed to the insurance company and thus become the company's bad faith.[44] However, under Georgia law, the potential liability of an insurance broker or agent (separate from the potential liability of the insurer itself) is limited to the terms of the

---

[40] *Greene v. Lilburn Ins. Agency*, 191 Ga. App. 829, 830, 383 S.E.2d 194 (1989), *citing McCullohs Service Station v. Wilkes*, 183 Ga. App. 687, 689-690 (1), 359 S.E.2d 745 (1987).

[41] *Westchester Specialty Insurance Services, Inc. v. U.S. Fire Insurance Company*, 119 F.3d 1505, 1510 (11th Cir. 1997).

[42] *Atlanta Women's Club, Inc. v. Washburne*, 207 Ga.App. 3, 4, 427 S.E.2d 18 (1992) ("Atlanta Women's Club I"), *citing Wright Body Works, supra* at 269 and *Turner, Wood & Smith, supra* at 215.

[43] *Atlanta Women's Club, supra* at 5 (citations omitted).

[44] *See Kansas City Life Ins. Co. v. Williams*, 62 Ga.App. 707, 9 S.E.2d 680, 683-684 (1940) (bad faith of company's agent in denying insured's payment of first premium on life insurance policy to such agent, who was authorized to collect such premium and deliver policy to insured, became company's bad faith when it refused to pay amount of policy after insured's death on ground that agent was never paid for policy.)

insurance policy it negligently failed to procure.[45] An agent who negligently fails to procure the requested coverage is liable for loss or damage to the limit of the agreed policy.[46]

In *J. Smith Lanier & Company v. Southeastern Forge, Inc.*, the Georgia Supreme Court clarified that an agent or broker who negligently fails to procure a policy is not necessarily subject to the same law as an insurer who refuses to pay a claim in bad faith. Southeastern Forge was a client of the independent insurance broker J. Smith Lanier ("Lanier"). In 1998, Lanier prepared Southeastern's application for primary and excess general liability coverage, but negligently failed to list an event on the application when it was submitted to the excess insurer. After an agricultural blade manufactured by Southeastern Forge malfunctioned and injured a worker in Texas, the excess insurer sought a declaratory judgment that the policy was void *ab initio* for the failure to list the event on the application. Southeastern Forge then filed suit against Lanier, asserting negligence, breach of fiduciary duty, and breach of contract to recover the funds expended in the Texas suit. The trial court held that Southeastern Forge could not obtain more than the $2 million policy limits. The Georgia Supreme Court agreed, noting that under the facts of that case the law did not impose "the unique statutory duties of insurers on independent brokers who do not issue contracts of insurance and have no duty or ability to evaluate and compromise claims."[47]

---

[45] *J. Smith Lanier & Company v. Southeastern Forge, Inc.*, 280 Ga. 508, 509, 630 S.E.2d 404 (2006).

[46] *Id.*, citing *Beiter v. Decatur Fed. Savings & Loan Assoc.*, 222 Ga. 516, 518(2), 150 S.E.2d 687 (1966). *See also Home Bldg. &c. v. Hester*, 213 Ga. 393, 99 S.E.2d 87 (1957); *Case v. R.GA Ins. Svcs.*, 239 Ga. App. 1 (3), 521 S.E.2d 32 (1999); *Robinson v. J. Smith Lanier & Co.*, 220 Ga. App. 737 (1), 470 S.E.2d 272 (1996); *Clark, Davis & Easley Ins. Agency v. Tile Technology*, 217 Ga. App. 809, 459 S.E.2d 450 (1995); Moseley v. Coastal Plains Gin Co., 199 Ga. App. 99 (1)(a), 404 S.E.2d 123 (1991); Ga. Farm Bureau Mut. Ins. Co. v. Arnold, 175 Ga. App. 850, 850(1), 334 S.E.2d 733 (1985); *Beavers Ins. Agency v. Roland*, 135 Ga. App. 263, 217 S.E.2d 484 (1975).

[47] *Id.* at 510.

§ 7.6   STATUTE OF LIMITATION

A claim for negligent procurement is likely subject to the four-year statute of limitations.[48] Because the "action in tort for negligence depends upon the presence of damages and, therefore, may not be maintained until the principal suffers a loss," the statute of limitations for negligent procurement of insurance may not begin to run until the insurer denies coverage.[49]

---

[48] See, *Hoffman v. Ins. Co. of N. Am.*, 144 Ga. App. 420, 421, 241 S.E.2d 303, 304 (1977) (applying four-year limitation period), *rev'd on other grounds*, 241 Ga. 328, 245 S.E.2d 287 (1978) (ruling that statute of limitation did not begin running until loss experienced, but not addressing limitation period).

[49] See previous note and *Saye v. UnumProvident Corp.*, 2007 WL 2331050, *5 (N.D. Ga. 2007).